# Physical Characteristics of the Chinese Crested

## (from the American Kennel Club breed standard)

**Tail:** Slender and tapers to a curve. It is long enough to reach the hock. When dog is in motion, the tail is carried gaily and may be carried slightly forward over the back. In the Hairless variety, two-thirds of the end of the tail is covered by long, flowing feathering referred to as a plume.

**Topline:** Level to slightly sloping croup.

**Body:** Brisket extends to the elbow. Breastbone is not prominent. Ribs are well developed. The depth of the chest tapers to a moderate tuck-up at the flanks. Light in loin.

**Hindquarters:** Stifle moderately angulated. From hock joint to ground perpendicular.

**Coat:** The Hairless variety has hair on certain portions of the body: the head (called a crest), the tail (called a plume) and the feet from the toes to the front pasterns and rear hock joints (called socks). The texture of all hair is soft and silky, flowing to any length. Wherever the body is hairless, the skin is soft and smooth.

**Size:** Ideally 11 to 13 inches.

**Color:** Any color or combination of colors.

**Feet:** Hare foot
are trimmed to n

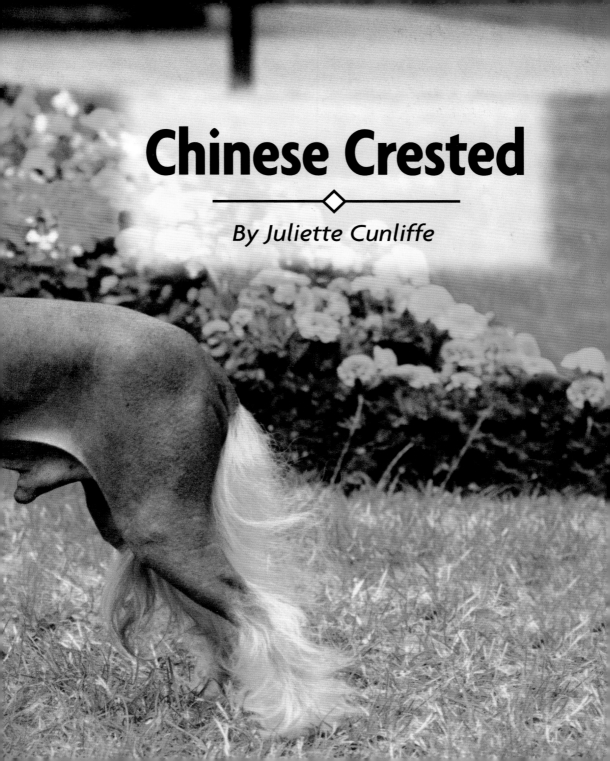

# Chinese Crested

By Juliette Cunliffe

# tents

## 9     History of the Chinese Crested

Trace the origins of the hairless dogs back to 13th-century China, the land from which the delightful and enigmatic Chinese Crested derived. Discover the first importations into the US and Britain and meet some of the important early dogs. Learn about the breed's peculiarities regarding hairlessness, teeth, color, Powderpuffs and much more.

## 26     Characteristics of the Chinese Crested

Meet the delightful Chinese Crested and answer the question: "Why the Chinese Crested?" Read about the breed's dynamic personality, including the Crested's many assets and a few drawbacks, and find out about the breed's physical characteristics and health considerations, vital information that every new owner needs before acquiring this one-of-a-kind dog.

## 36     Breed Standard for the Chinese Crested

Learn the ideal physical appearance of a well-bred Chinese Crested by studying the description of the breed set forth in the American Kennel Club standard. Both show dogs and pets must possess key characteristics as outlined in the breed standard.

## 40     Your Puppy Chinese Crested

Find out about how to locate a well-bred Chinese Crested puppy. Discover which questions to ask the breeder and what to expect when visiting the litter. Prepare for your puppy-accessory shopping spree. Also discussed are home safety, the first trip to the vet, socialization and solving basic puppy problems.

## 70     Proper Care of Your Chinese Crested

Cover the specifics of taking care of your Chinese Crested every day: feeding for the puppy, adult and senior dog; grooming, including skin and coat care, ears, nails and bathing; and exercise needs for your dog. Also discussed are the essentials of dog identification.

KENNEL CLUB BOOKS: **CHINESE CRESTED**
ISBN: 1-59378-305-1

Copyright © 2005 • Kennel Club Books, LLC
308 Main Street, Allenhurst, NJ 07711 USA
Cover Design Patented: US 6,435,559 B2 • Printed in South Korea

Photography by Isabelle Français and Carol Ann Johnson
with additional photographs by

Paulette Braun, T.J. Calhoun, Alan and Sandy Carey, Carolina Biological Supply, David Dalton, J C Photo, Bill Jonas, Dr. Dennis Kunkel, Tam C. Nguyen, Phototake and Jean Claude Revy.

Illustrations by Patricia Peters.

The publisher wishes to thank all of the owners whose dogs are illustrated in this book, including Arlene Butterklee, Victor Helu, Cindy Kumpfbeck, Mrs. A. and Miss T. McGuigan, Carol and Paul Mount and Sande Weigand.

Speculation, fiction and novelty abound in the history of the Chinese Crested and the other hairless breeds.

# CHINESE CRESTED

### ORIGIN OF THE BREED

If there were a definite answer to where the Chinese Crested actually originated, undoubtedly many authors would be very happy. However, the Chinese Crested's history is a matter that has been the subject of speculation and debate, with almost more fiction than fact in its background.

The breed is certainly a distinctive one, but there are other hairless breeds, and the histories of various similar breeds may have been confused. The Chinese Crested, as we know it today, appeared in China's written history as long ago as the 13th century. Indeed, it is probable that the breed existed in that country long before then. Chinese seafarers and traders visited many places on their travels, and hairless dogs later appeared in many of their ports of call. Hairless dogs were certainly also mentioned in the chronicles of Christopher Columbus and the later Conquistadors.

It is possible that such dogs were kept on ships in order to control vermin, though, unhappily, they might also have been a source of food. Hairless dogs were undoubtedly found in both Asia and Africa during the 18th and 19th centuries. However, a similar dog was also found in Mexico and in Central and South America in the 16th century. This dog was known as the Xoloitzcuintli; it is still known by that name or, alternatively, as the Mexican Hairless, and is registered as a different breed from the Chinese Crested. While there are obvious similarities between the two breeds, there are indeed differences. Even within the breed, Xoloitzcuintli vary tremendously in size.

An important question arises, though, about whether the Chinese obtained their dogs from the Central and South American regions, or whether seafarers took along their

**THE CHINESE CRESTED IN ART**
There are several examples of the Chinese Crested's appearance in works of art. Going back to the 15th century, a painting by Gerrard Davies titled *Christ Nailed to the Cross* includes a hairless dog very similar to the Chinese Crested breed we know today.

Another painting of note is one painted by Jacques Laurent Agasse (1767–1849). This depicts a male Crested, clearly of the deer type. As with some of the engravings found in 19th-century canine works, the dog shown in the painting would not find himself out of place in today's show ring.

A modern Xoloitzcuintli, also known as the Mexican Hairless.

Illustration of a Chinese Crested in the early 19th century. The Crested was cited as "one of the most unusual in appearance" among the hairless breeds found in various parts of the world at that time.

## PURE-BRED PURPOSE

Surely domestic dogs are the most versatile animal in the kingdom. From the tiny 1-pound lap dog to the 200-pound guard dog, dogs have adapted to every need and whim of their human masters. Humans have select-ively bred dogs to alter physical attributes like size, color, leg length, mass and skull diameter in order to suit our own needs and fancies. Dogs serve humans not only as companions and guardians but also as hunters, exterminators, shepherds, rescuers, messengers, warriors, babysitters and more!

own Chinese dogs to those lands, using them there for trade and barter. Perhaps one day the facts will be discovered but, to date, there is no conclusive evidence one way or the other.

### THE NINETEENTH CENTURY

The first Chinese Cresteds in Britain, brought to that country in the 1860s, were placed in zoological collections, and no serious attempt was made to breed from them; instead, they were treated as fascinating novelties. In the book *Dogs of the British Isles*, published in 1867, we read that the variety of

An engraving of a Chinese Crested Dog in the 19th century.

Engraving titled "Hairless Dog" from *A Book of Beasts and Birds*, published in 1893.

same strain." Because of its very affectionate disposition, it was believed that, if the breed could be developed, it would please many as something of a "novelty pet."

Several early canine writers maintained that the Chinese Crested Dog was the same dog as the African Sand Dog and the hairless

> **HAIRLESS BREEDS**
> There are many other hairless breeds of dog besides the Chinese Crested. Over the span of time these have included the Abyssinian or African Sand Dog, African Elephant Dog, Buenos Aires Hairless, Guatemalan Hairless, Inca Orchid, Nubian Dog, Peruvian Hairless, Small African Greyhound, Turkish Hairless, Xoloitzcuintli or Mexican Hairless and Zulu Sand Dog.

Chinese dog furnished with a crest and tufted tail was by no means common. The dog's skin was described as spotted, and it was estimated that there were between 12 and 18 hairs on the surface of the body, thus making the tufts on the two extremities even more remark-able. It is interesting that 19th-century illustrations show the Chinese Crested with no tufts of longer hair on the feet. Indeed, most pictures of such dogs in the 1800s showed no hair in this area.

The bitch portrayed in *Dogs of the British Isles* was two years old in 1866 and was the only surviving puppy from a litter of six. When the book was written, she had never been bred from, due to the difficulty in finding a suitable male "of the

dogs of both Mexico and Japan. However, they did comment that the Chinese Crested had to have a crest on the top of the head and on the tail, something not common to all

such breeds. The African Sand Dog also had a crest but, at least in those exhibited, it was shorter and much harsher than those of the Chinese Crested.

## THE EARLY TWENTIETH CENTURY

As the 20th century turned, we find the Chinese Crested described as an "outlandish" breed of "rather a rare sort." Charles Henry Lane, a prominent show judge of the day, wrote that, although he had judged Foreign Dog classes at all of the leading shows, there had been very few specimens of this scarce breed exhibited under him.

The best Chinese Crested that Lane had ever seen was called Chinese Emperor, owned by Mr. W. K. Taunton. He commented that the tuft of stiffish hair, either on the forehead or above it, was usually nearly white or a "whitey brown" in color, as was the tuft on the top end of the tail. In shape and style of body, the breed resembled a coarse, strong Italian Greyhound, but the Chinese Crested nearly always gave one the impression of its being adversely affected by the cold! In Lane's view, this was not a breed suitable for the climate of Britain, unless in what he termed "favourable circumstances," and he had never heard of their being used for anything other than companions and pets.

In 1903 W. D. Drury, writing in the book *British Dogs*, referred to

### CANIS LUPUS

"Grandma, what big teeth you have!" The gray wolf, a familiar figure in fairy tales and legends, has had its reputation tarnished and its population pummeled over the centuries. Yet it is the descendants of this much-feared creature to which we open our homes and hearts. Our beloved dog, *Canis domesticus*, derives directly from the gray wolf, a highly social canine that lives in elaborately structured packs. In the wild, the gray wolf can range from 60 to 175 pounds, standing between 25 and 40 inches in height.

Chinese Cresteds as terriers. He commented on the great variance in size within the breed, from 10 pounds up to as much as 25 pounds, saying that in recent years he had found them of varying quality. He even advised prospective purchasers to make certain that they were buying a genuine hairless dog, not a terrier without hair. In his opinion, any appearance of tan on the legs and feet suggested a cross of Black-and-Tan Terrier blood.

The Chinese Crested's skin was expected to be bluish in color, resembling the color of an elephant's hide. Although the skin was frequently mottled, this

H. C. Brooke's Mexican Hairless, Paderewski Junior, circa 1907. This dog was famous during his time for his intelligence and hunting ability.

## THE BREED NAME

The Chinese Crested Dog has had several different names bestowed on it over the years; among these are Chinese Hairless, Chinese Ship Dog and Chinese Royal Hairless. It is even said that the breed was called the Chinese Edible Dog, though, in this author's experience, this name usually refers to the Chow Chow.

In Egypt the Chinese Crested has been called Pyramid, or Giza, Hairless, while in South Africa the breed has been known as South African Hairless. Very similar, but slightly larger, dogs in Turkey have been called Turkish Hairless.

apparently was not considered correct at that time.

Perhaps the temptation of the 19th- and early 20th-century canine writers to link the hairless breeds with terriers had something to do with the dogs' gameness. In 1904, Herbert Compton treats readers of his book *The Twentieth Century Dog* to what he calls "a not altogether happy-looking little animal" by the name of Paderewski Junior, a Mexican Hairless. He and his father, Hairy King (who was, incidentally, captioned "Chinese Crested Dog" in the 1903 *British Dogs*), were splendid ratters, and Junior was considered exceptionally intelligent and game. He would hunt rabbits in company with a pack of Beagles, and could face gorse as well as, if

An engraving from 1791 of the "Naked Turkish Dog."

not better than, the hounds.

By 1907 the Chinese Crested, along with other hairless breeds, still created some attention in canine publications; these dogs were, after all, something of a curiosity. The size of hairless dogs in Britain varied between as little as around 4 to 5 lbs to as much as 25 lbs. There were two types. One was

Like the breed's
ancestors, today's
Chinese Crested is
a remarkable
sight.

built along the lines of the Manchester Terrier, sometimes attaining the racy fineness of a Whippet, while the other was short-legged and cloddy. The latter was said to be "decidedly unpleasant in appearance; its bareness giving the impression of disease, added to which it was prone to ungainly obesity." It was, however, recognized that some specimens were very active and remarkably intelligent.

**"REGISTERING" FOR CHINESE CRESTEDS**
Dating back to the 15th century, five Chinese Cresteds were included in an inventory of wedding gifts.

**TEETH IN HAIRLESS BREEDS**
Even during the breed's early recognition in Britain, it was noted that the dentition of the Chinese Cresteds was abnormal and imperfect. Darwin had said that, in most animals, the teeth and horns had some relation to growth or absence of hair. Bald mammals seldom had large horns or tusks, while long-coated ones, such as Highland cattle, wild boars and even the hairy mammoth, were remarkable for their horns or tusks.

**SKIN AND LACK OF COAT GROWTH**
Many of the early authors who wrote about the hairless breeds considered that their countries' dry climates might have had some effect at least in producing dogs without hair. The dogs' skin was usually extremely delicate and, unless smeared with grease, blistered in the summer if exposed to the sun.

By the early 1930s, one notable canine encyclopedia said that hairless dogs could only be looked upon as "freaks" due to the absence of certain bodies in their blood. It was also noted that some of the dogs had top-knots, and an interesting comparison was drawn with the human race—also relatively hairless, even though the hair on the head could grow to a considerable length.

## HAIRLESS DOGS CROSSED WITH OTHER BREEDS

A century or more ago, perhaps for the sake of curiosity or perhaps because of the difficulty in finding compatible members of their own

The bluish skin color, resembling that of an elephant's hide, was mentioned in early 19th-century descriptions of the Chinese Crested.

kind, several crosses were made between hairless dogs and other breeds.

A Fox Terrier bitch was once mated to Hairy King, apparently because her owner needed to use the bitch as a foster mother for Bull Terrier puppies. Of the puppies produced by the mating, several puppies looked like fair specimens of Fox Terrier, but two of them were especially weird-looking creatures. They had Fox Terrier heads but were hairless. Their skin was mottled along the body to the hips where, on each side, was a tuft of hair about the size of a half dollar piece. The tail was bare from its root to the middle, but the end was like that of a Fox Terrier, and, while the

Ch. Gingery's Truffles 'N' Cream CD, owned by Arleen Butterklee, was the Top Crested in 1987. At seven years of age, Truffles was the oldest Crested to receive an AKC Championship. She won a Best in Show prior to AKC recognition and is the dam of Ch. Gingery's Cheesecake.

**WHAT CAUSES THAT?**
Over the centuries there has been much debate about the cause of hairlessness in dogs. Some thought it was caused by a deficiency in the dogs' diets, while others believed that climatic conditions in the countries where the dogs were found affected them. Hairless dogs sent to London's Zoological Gardens were carefully examined, but no significant discovery was made.

legs were bare to the knee joint, the feet also resembled those of a terrier.

## A WORD ABOUT THE MEXICAN DOGS

The Mexican Hairless was usually of a uniform color and, though some described it as being "of greyhound type," it was only about 18 pounds in weight. The breed was said to have been used externally on humans to ease the symptoms of rheumatism and, unfortunately, also internally to allay the pangs of hunger! So clearly both the Chinese and the Aztecs included the canine species in their diets.

The hairless dogs of Mexico were good guards and also popular as pet dogs, having the advantage of being practically free from fleas.

## CHINESE CRESTEDS IN THE US

In 1880 Ida Garret, a young New Yorker, became interested in the Chinese Crested dog. She became so

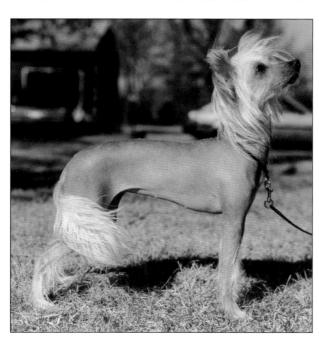

enthusiastically involved with the breed that she not only bred and exhibited Chinese Cresteds but also wrote about them. Some years later, in the 1920s, Garret had befriended Debra Woods of Florida and also became involved with the breed. Together, they promoted the Chinese Crested in the US in the first half of the 20th century.

Debra Woods kept a logbook of all her own dogs, which she bred under the name "Crest Haven." By the 1950s, this logbook was sufficiently extensive for her to begin a registration service for the breed and to establish the American Hairless Dog Club (AHDC). The AHDC became the main registering body for all breeds of dogs in the US that had a hairless variety.

In the 1950s the world-famous entertainer and strip-tease artist Gypsy Rose Lee was given her first Chinese Crested (named Fu Man Chu) by her sister, the actress June Havoc. Miss Lee became a devoted breeder of Chinese Cresteds and used her fame to promote the breed wherever she traveled. Nearly all the American lines can trace their origins to dogs bred by either Debra Woods and/or Gypsy Rose Lee.

Although the American Kennel Club (AKC) has documented Chinese Crested entries in shows as early as the late 1800s, the breed was not fully recognized by AKC. In fact, there was a Chinese Crested entered in the Miscellaneous Class at the ninth annual Westminster

Not all Chinese Crested Dogs are hairless. The coated variety, known as the Powderpuff, is otherwise basically identical to the Hairless, with only minor differences.

Kennel Club Show in 1885, exactly 100 years before the breed was admitted into the AKC Miscellaneous Class.

The American Chinese Crested Club (ACCC) was founded in 1979 with one of its goals being to have the breed accepted into the AKC Stud Book and able to compete for Best in Show. The ACCC held its first annual meeting on June 1, 1980. Under the guidance of then ACCC president S. M. "Dick" Dickerson, the club and the breed thrived and improved. In September 1985, the breed entered the Miscellaneous Class, in which the breed could compete in conformation shows (without earning championships) as well as participate in obedience trials. It didn't take long for Dickerson's Hop Sing to become the breed's first Companion Dog titleholder. The first Powderpuff to earn the title was Miclanjo Ki-Mi Wagayo, owned by Michael and Marie Mooney. The ACCC realized its goal on April 1, 1991, when the first Chinese Cresteds entered the Toy Group and was eligible to compete for the title Champion.

The Stud Book, began by Debra Woods in the 1950s, was passed on to Jo Ann Orlick upon Mrs. Woods's death in 1969 and then became the property of the ACCC in 1979. The AKC took over the Stud Book in November 1990 and continues to

### LITTLE JADE

In the 13th century there was a description of a Chinese Crested called Little Jade. This fortunate little dog apparently had jade beads plaited into its mane, and these plaits were threaded with gold and silver. Little Jade also had a fur-lined coat for cold weather.

maintain it. Today there are thousands of Cresteds registered every year.

While there were many individuals who worked hard and supported the breed and its parent

**No longer frowned upon by Chinese Crested fanciers, the Powderpuffs are essential members of the breed.**

club during these years, only a few remain today who have been active for more than 20 years and have contributed significantly to the breed.

At the top of the list, of course, is Arlene Butterklee, who established Gingery Chinese Cresteds in Ronkonkoma, NY in the early 1980s. Although she started off breeding "as a hobby," Arleen fast became one of the most influential Chinese Crested people in the US. The Gingery line was developed from the Gipez and Xcel lines and quickly became known for its exquisite beauty and its competitiveness in the breed ring. While most people were showing the Hairless variety only, Arleen was one of the few fanciers who were actively exhibiting both varieties. In the breed ring, the depth of her accomplishments is not easily equaled. Gingery Chinese Cresteds won the first five Best of Breed awards at the prestigious Westminster Kennel Club Show: Powderpuff Ch. Gingery's Maple Syrup (1992–1993) and Hairless Ch. Gingery's Brandywine (1994–1996). That a Powderpuff won the first two Westminster awards is worthy of notice, as the variety was not favored in these early years. To add to Arleen's distinctions, she is the only breeder and owner in the US of Best in Show winners of both varieties and can claim Sires and Dams of Distinction in both varieties.

The winner of the first two Westminster Best of Breed awards, Ch. Gingery's Maple Syrup was the #2 Chinese Crested and #1 Powderpuff in 1991–1992. He was the only Powderpuff to win multiple Best in Show awards and was the first Sire of Distinction. He also was the first to win an agility title. Owner, Arleen Butterklee.

Although Gingery dogs are very competitive in conformation shows, Arlene is credited with demonstrating the versatility of the Chinese Crested by proving that this breed could do more than the early exhibitors ever believed. Long before AKC recognition, she was the first in the breed to get Chinese Cresteds involved in other activities, including obedience, agility and therapy work. Arlene believed there was nothing that this breed could not do. Today, her Chinese Cresteds are also used in activities ranging from Flyball competitions to hearing-ear dog work for the deaf.

ACCC charter member and former officer Jean Scott (Luvan Chinese Cresteds) of Tennessee owned the first Chinese Crested to be awarded an AKC Best in Show. Ch. Darshire Sun Nee Dal of Luvan was awarded BIS less than a week after the breed was accepted into the AKC.

Lejo Chinese Cresteds of Pennsylvania (owned by Lee Bakuckas, a charter member and

Whether Powderpuff or Hairless, the Chinese Crested can be seen in any color or combination of colors. The skin of the Hairless is often mottled.

former vice president of the ACCC) started in the breed with dogs from the original Phaedrian line. ACCC Ch. Lejo's Halo of Phadrean, shown in the 1980s, was one of the most beautiful bitches in the US and went on to produce many champions of quality. Lejo Chinese Cresteds are still actively competing, promoting both varieties in conformation and obedience.

Jan Poe, also a charter member of the ACCC, established Xcel Chinese Cresteds and preserved the breed in the original form. While producing elegant dogs that were truly hairless, her focus has always been porcelain skin and superior front assemblies. Xcel kennel did not give into the pressure of shaving down semi-hairless dogs; instead,

### PIGTAILS OR PIG TALE?

It is sometimes said that the crest of hair on top of the Chinese Crested's head is reminiscent of a Chinese pigtail, as worn in the past by the men of China. Who knows?

through selective breeding, Jan worked and kept the original Chinese Crested characteristics that make this breed so special.

Victor Helu (Victory Chinese Cresteds) of New York acquired his first Chinese Crested from Arlene Butterklee in the early 1980s. Although he was one of the top three breeders in 1991 (and he rarely used his kennel name), Victor stopped breeding for a number of years so that he could concentrate on promoting the Powderpuff variety in the conformation ring. During the early years of AKC recognition, the Hairless variety enjoyed tremendous popularity within the breed at the expense of the Powderpuff variety. Alarmed that the Powderpuff risked obscurity and the breed

The high-set, large ears complement the breed's quizzical expression. A fringe on the ears, when present, adds to the Crested's elegance.

would suffer, he successfully campaigned a female Powderpuff, Ch. Gingery's Cheesecake, for three years ranking her as the #2 Chinese Crested. Largely due to efforts of people like Victor, the Powderpuff variety can be shown successfully in a breed in which the varieties are not separated.

The breed is now well known at shows throughout America, and there are several regional clubs affiliated with the ACCC. The ACCC does some very important work in looking after the breed, including sponsoring a confidential health survey which compiles information regarding health and genetic issues of the Chinese Crested. The completed survey is used to prioritize research targeted to improve the overall health and sturdiness of the breed.

Undoubtedly the American people have now taken this wonderful and unusual breed to the very center of their hearts. Today American breed enthusiasts boast

all sorts of breed memorabilia and deck themselves in sweatshirts and tee shirts with Chinese Crested designs emblazoned on front and back. There is even a design of a Chinese Crested against the American flag. Yes, this special little breed has certainly won over the American dog-lover, just as it has the dog fraternity around the rest of the world.

### GYPSY ROSE LEE

Gypsy Rose Lee, the famous American singer, dancer and entertainer, was greatly involved with promoting the Chinese Crested breed throughout the world. Her sister, the actress June Havoc, had obtained a Chinese Crested from an animal shelter in Connecticut and presented the dog to Ms. Lee in the 1950s. Many of today's dogs can be traced back to Ms. Lee's breeding.

## CRESTEDS IN THE UK

We know that there had been Chinese and other hairless dogs in Britain before, but it was not until 1881 that the first Chinese Crested Dog was actually registered in Britain. At that time, there was attention paid by the English Kennel Club to the two distinct types of Chinese Crested—"deer" and "cobby"—the latter being heavier in body and bone than the former, which was, and indeed still is, racy and fine-boned.

Although the breed had appeared in England in small numbers from time to time, it was December 2, 1965 that heralded the beginning of Britain's modern-day Chinese Cresteds. America's Debra Woods exported the bitch Alto to Mrs. Ruth Harris of the Staround kennels in Britain. Alto arrived in whelp, but sadly her puppies did not survive. However, this reputedly sound bitch with erect ears was shown at Championship Shows in the Any Variety classes, and she was featured not only in the newspapers but also on television and radio.

The following year, Mrs. Harris imported two bitches, Brittas and Eloa, and a dog, Nero, from the same source. In the late 1960s, other dogs and bitches came in from the Crest Haven kennels. In 1969 the popular entertainer Gypsy Rose Lee brought over three Chinese Cresteds of different bloodlines from her own kennels.

More Chinese Cresteds were imported into Britain during the 1970s, but not all of them came from the US. All were hairless, but litters sired by hairless parents can include coated puppies. It was clear that the Lee and Crest Haven lines, mated together, produced not only stronger bodies but also heavier crests and plumes. More and more people showed an interest in the breed, and soon demand outstripped supply.

The Chinese Crested is now fairly well scattered in show rings across the globe, though numbers and quality vary from country to country. The breed was first imported into Australia in 1975; that country has had an ardent band of Chinese Crested followers ever since.

## POWDERPUFFS

Although coated Chinese Cresteds, known as Powderpuffs, were known from the early days of the breed in Britain, for several years after the foundation of the Chinese Crested Dog Club in 1969 such specimens were frowned upon. Members of the club were actually asked to neither breed from them nor register them with the British Kennel Club. There was indeed much debate as to what should actually be done with them! Some thought it would be best to try to develop them as a separate breed, whereas others believed it would be better to cull them.

Although Powderpuffs appeared in litters produced from two hairless parents, there was considerable difference in type among the coated puppies produced. Some could be as tall as 17 inches, while others were very small; yet others were of suitable size and quality to compete with the coated specimens of the breed found in the show ring today.

In the early 1970s, at a breed club annual general meeting, it was passed that "Hair on any other part of the body other than stated in the standard" was a disqualifying fault. But time has moved on—in the 1980s opinions were modified and the standard was changed so that now the Powderpuff is regularly exhibited alongside hairless dogs in the same class.

The Powderpuff's ears may be dropped or erect, while the ears of the Hairless must be erect. This Powderpuff shows erect ears with lovely black fringe.

# CHINESE CRESTED

### WHY THE CHINESE CRESTED?

This graceful, elegant breed is frequently described as a little prancing pony, or sometimes as a fawn in miniature. The Chinese Crested is a small dog, and the Hairless variety requires minimal coat care. The coated variety, called the Powderpuff, requires a little more grooming, but nothing like the amount of time one needs to devote to the heavily coated breeds such as the Shih Tzu and Lhasa Apso. Both Hairless and Powderpuff Chinese Cresteds are shown in the same classes and are judged by the same breed standard. The appearance of the Hairless variety does not, understandably, appeal to everyone, but those who like the breed are usually head over heels about this fun-loving, affectionate companion.

### PERSONALITY

This is a happy breed, one that should never be vicious, although it can be a little feisty and will not be put upon by other dogs. Tremendous fun around the home, the Chinese Crested usually enjoys the company of other pets and thoroughly enjoys family life,

Puppy meets cat! Although small, the Chinese Crested can certainly hold his own and usually gets along well with other family pets.

in which he participates enthusiastically. This is a breed that loves to be with its owners, whether inside or outside the house. With their skin that is warm to the

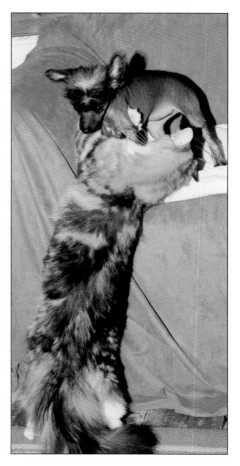

touch, more than a few enjoy acting as 'hot-water bottles' on cold nights! In the past it was claimed that the breed could 'cure' arthritis, though perhaps today that would be considered a little far-fetched.

The Chinese Crested is not a dog that should be left alone for long periods of time, for he enjoys company too much. When in the mood for love, he adores being cuddled and is affectionate in return. Due to their affectionate nature and intelligence, some Chinese Cresteds have been used in therapy work.

This is an agile breed that thoroughly enjoys play, but its small size must be taken into consideration; excessive "rough-and-tumble" is not advised. Like most other breeds of dog, the Chinese Crested can enjoy the company of children, but it is essential that small children are always supervised with dogs and that they are taught to treat them with respect.

Because the Chinese Crested can be rather shy, socialization is very important. Without this, there is a danger of the Chinese Crested's becoming rather nervous and over-protective of his most treasured human friends. It is important, therefore, to devote plenty of time to the breed, which is exceptionally intelligent and is usually ready to learn basic obedience commands. Provided

**PUFF DADDIES**

The coated Chinese Crested, known as the Powderpuff, can be produced as the result of a mating of two Hairless dogs, or of a Hairless mated with a Powderpuff. Both of these combinations can produce either coat type. However, a Powderpuff mated to another Powderpuff will only produce its own kind.

that training is made interesting, and that the dog can see a point in the exercise, training can be relatively easy. The breed can, though, be rather stubborn at times.

The Chinese Crested is viewed as somewhat of a primitive breed, and some individuals have a tendency to mark their territory just as their ancestors did. This applies to both

**Chinese Cresteds love to be with their owners wherever they go!**

dogs and bitches. They also make fairly good watchdogs and are not afraid to use their barks, so firm control in this area from the outset is a wise thing. The Chinese Crested will always let its owners know when someone has arrived at the door, but will generally quiet down when the visitor has been welcomed.

**PHYSICAL CHARACTERISTICS**
Small, active and graceful dogs, their bone varies between fine and medium, for there are two distinct types. One is type is known as "deer" and is racy and fine-boned; the other is known as "cobby" and is heavier in both bone and bodily structure.

Both types have a very distinctive extreme hare-foot, which should be long and narrow. There is a unique elongation of the small bones between the joints, so that the feet appear almost to have an extra joint, although actually they do not. The dog's nails are kept fairly long as well. The feet of the Chinese Crested have sometimes been likened to hands, for the dogs are quite capable of curling up their feet to grasp and hold objects, in a rather prehensile fashion.

With his slightly rounded and elongated skull, the Chinese Crested has cleanly chiseled cheeks that taper into the muzzle. The eyes are so dark as to appear black, and the nose is a prominent

**HEART-HEALTHY**
In this modern age of ever-improving cardio-care, no doctor or scientist can dispute the advantages of owning a dog to lower a person's risk of heart disease. Studies have proven that petting a dog, walking a dog and grooming a dog all show positive results toward lowering your blood pressure. The simple routine of exercising your dog—going outside with the dog and walking, jogging or playing catch—is heart-healthy in and of itself. If you are normally less active than your physician thinks you should be, adopting a dog may be a smart option to improve your own quality of life as well as that of another creature.

## HOT-WATER BOTTLE
The Hairless Chinese Crested has a body that is warm to the touch. Its temperature is 104°F, as opposed to 101-102°F, the temperature of most other breeds. It comes as no surprise, then, that the breed is sometimes deservedly known as a walking hot-water bottle.

feature, being narrow in keeping with the muzzle.

### SIZE
The size of the breed can vary quite considerably in both height and weight. Males should ideally measure 11–13 inches at the withers, while bitches are 9–12 inches. In accordance with the variance in both height and bone structure, weight is variable, but should not exceed 12 pounds.

### SKIN AND COAT
Another very obvious difference in the breed is that of coat, for two types of coat can be produced in the very same litter. One type has a smooth hairless body, with hair on the feet, head and tail only; the other, known as the Powderpuff, has an undercoat with a soft veil of long hair, the veil coat being a distinct feature of this type.

On the Hairless dogs, the skin is fine-grained, smooth and warm to the touch. Perhaps surprisingly, it does not scratch easily. However, owners should be aware

Hairless or Powderpuff, the Chinese Crested attracts attention from viewers everywhere.

of the fact that the skin can burn in sunlight and, whatever the weather, a little baby oil, lotion or a suitable moisturizer should be applied to the skin to keep it soft and supple. One of the advantages of the naked variety is that it is highly unlikely to harbor fleas! There is also no doggy odor, nor indeed any dandruff, so Chinese Crested makes a good pet for a

**The Powderpuff coat on a five-month-old puppy.**

**TALKNG TYPE**

The type of Chinese Crested now referred to as the "cobby" type was once called the "Hunting Dog." The others, which we now call "deer" type, were known as the "Treasure House Guardians."

house-proud owner.

Although known as "Hairless," even the hairless dogs have some hair. This should be restricted to the tail, feet and head, where the crest ideally begins at the stop and tapers off down the neck. Although a long, flowing crest is preferred, a sparse one is acceptable. The plume on the tail is restricted to the lower two-thirds but, again, a sparse plume is acceptable. The coat on the feet is referred to as "socks," and these ideally should be confined to the toes and should never extend above the top of the pastern. In theory, Hairless Chinese Cresteds should have no hair on their bodies, but some do grow a minimal amount of hair. In this case, the small amount of body hair simply will need to be tidied up.

The Powderpuff variety is the same dog as the Hairless variety other than in coat and in occasional minor differences in dentition, ear carriage and, according to some owners, personality.

## COLOR

The Chinese Cresteds may be any color or combination of colors, allowing for a wide range, both plain and spotted. Frequently, spotted dogs are pink all over when born, and spots begin to appear after about a week. The spots initially appear as pin-sized dots, gradually increasing with the progression of time. In summer, the color has a tendency to deepen.

The variety of colors found in this very special little breed of dog include white, pink, blue and copper, among many others. A puppy that is born black may well

The Chinese Crested is not special *only* for his looks. He's a small dog packed with personality, intelligence and affection.

turn out silver, white or even tri-colored by the time he has reached maturity. In Powderpuffs the coat color may change with maturity, sometimes becoming lighter with age.

## TEETH

The Chinese Crested should have a strong jaw, with teeth closing in a scissors bite, meaning that the upper incisors closely overlap the lower ones. In Powderpuffs breeders expect full dentition, but Hairless Chinese Cresteds frequently have fewer teeth. Sometimes the canines face forward in the Hairless, in which

## DELTA SOCIETY

The human-animal bond propels the work of the Delta Society, striving to improve the lives of people and animals. The Pet Partners Program proves that the lives of people and dogs are inextricably linked. The Pet Partners Program, a national registry, trains and screens volunteers for pet therapy in hospices, nursing homes, schools and rehabilitation centers. Dog-and-handler teams of Pet Partners volunteer in all 50 states, with nearly 7,000 teams making visits annually. About 900,000 patients, residents and students receive assistance each year. If you and your dog are interested in becoming Pet Partners, contact the Delta Society online at www.deltasociety.org.

The size, set and fringe of the Crested's ears add splendor to an already magnificent looking breed.

case the teeth are known as "tusks." Hairless Chinese Cresteds typically have missing premolars.

### TOENAILS
Toenails on the Chinese Crested are kept moderately long, and on occasion a Hairless may have missing toenails.

### EARS
The Chinese Crested's ears are large but set low, with the highest point of the base being level with the outside corner of the eye. They stand erect on all Hairless Chinese Cresteds, giving a rather quizzical expression, especially when fully alert. Hairless dogs often have a fringe on their ears, adding to the breed's splendor, but lack of fringing is not considered a fault. The ears on the Powderpuff may also stand erect,

but drop ears are also permissible in the coated variety.

### TAILS
On both the Hairless and Powderpuff varieties, the tail is set high and, when the dog is in motion, carried up or out. When the dog is at rest, the long, tapering tail falls naturally, neither curled nor twisted to either side.

### PECULIARITIES
In Chinese Cresteds, heat is released via sweat glands rather than by way of panting; panting is how most other breeds lower their temperatures when hot. Another rather unusual characteristic is that many act in a somewhat feline manner and, on occasion, clean themselves as a cat would.

## HEALTH CONSIDERATIONS IN THE BREED

In general, the Chinese Crested is a healthy breed. They are hardy little dogs, although, as has been mentioned, it is sensible to be aware of the potential danger of sunburn in hot weather. The Chinese Crested is a member of the Toy Group and, as such, can be prone to some of the medical problems encountered by other members of this group.

### LEGG-CALVE-PERTHES DISEASE

Legg-Calve-Perthes disease, or necrosis of the femoral head, is believed to be hereditary, as it seems to be noticed more in some family bloodlines than in others. It occurs more frequently in smaller breeds of dog than in larger ones. Initial lameness slowly becomes worse, eventually causing the dog to carry the affected limb. With time, due to disuse, the muscles of the thigh and upper leg disappear and the head of the femur becomes distorted. This condition can encourage further joint pain and osteoarthritis. Clearly, veterinary advice should be sought at the first sign of lameness.

### PATELLAR LUXATION

A problem from which some Chinese Cresteds can suffer is patellar luxation, which is trouble with the knee joints. A sign of this is when the dog limps or carries one leg off the ground when running. The dog does this because a bone has slipped out of position, due to either injury or poor alignment. It is important that a dog so affected is not allowed to become overweight, as that is likely to exacerbate the problem.

Many dogs with patellar luxation live with the problem without experiencing pain, but sometimes surgery is necessary. A veterinary testing procedure is available.

### PROGRESSIVE RETINAL ATROPHY (PRA)

Progressive retinal atrophy concerns breeders of Chinese Cresteds and they insist upon

---

## BLOCK THE SUN!

Chinese Crested are more sensitive to solar damage than are most other breeds, due to their obvious lack of coat and pink skin pigmentation. Though white-coated dogs prove to be equally at risk, the Chinese Crested has the advantage of having nice smooth skin on which to apply a sunscreen lotion (never less than SPF 15). Symptoms of sunburn include skin that is tender and painful, redness and, in bad cases, blisters and ulceration. Be certain to protect the dog's most sensitive body parts and avoid the dog's being outdoors during peak sun hours.

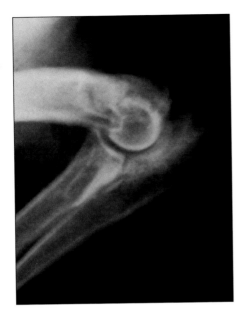
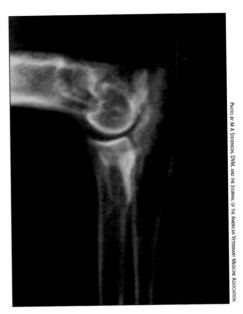

**X-ray diagnosis of elbow dysplasia in a three-and-a-half-year-old dog.**

having their stock tested for PRA. This is a hereditary eye disease that results in eventual blindness, caused by a breakdown of cells in the retina. The onset of blindness is usually slow, and an affected dog experiences no pain.

### Other Eye Problems

Some Chinese Cresteds are known to suffer from "dry eye" (kerato-conjunctivitis sicca), usually caused by a lack of tear production. There can be several reasons for this: lack of nerve stimulation near the lachrymal glands, malfunction of the tear glands or blockage of tear ducts.

In dogs thus affected, the eyes themselves are dry and lack their usual luster. This problem can be controlled with the application of artificial "tears," but veterinary guidance should always be sought to determine the cause.

Some owners shave the eyelashes of their Chinese Cresteds, and these, too, can cause a problem as they grow back in.

### Problems with Hair Follicles

True hairless dogs can get little "hooks" in the skin, caused by the hairs' being unable to grow. Should this happen, the little "hooks" will need to be taken out.

### Tooth Loss

The Chinese Crested has a tendency to lose its teeth sooner than many other breeds, and this is especially prevalent in the

Hairless variety. This gives owners all the more reason for always carefully checking their dogs' teeth, keeping them as clean as possible.

**ACNE AND OTHER SKIN PROBLEMS**
Hairless Chinese Cresteds are susceptible to having blackheads and pimples. It is therefore essential that their skin is kept thoroughly clean, and routine grooming is important, despite their lack of coat.

Some suffer from acne during the equivalent of a human's "teenage" stage of development, but they usually grow out of it. Veterinary assistance can be of help, and some owners have found that a five- or six-week course of antibiotics can solve the

**FREE WHELPERS**
Unlike some of the more exaggerated breeds, the Chinese Crested is what is known as a "free whelper." Veterinary assistance is rarely required during the whelping process but, of course, as with any other dog, complications can arise from time to time, so breeders should always be prepared as whelping time approaches.

problem. Clearly, though, it is always wiser to find solutions without the use of antibiotics if at all possible.

**WOOL AND LANOLIN ALLERGIES**
A high proportion of Chinese Cresteds are allergic to woolen items or products that contain wool. For this reason, woolen sweaters and the like cannot be used for this breed. Likewise, one should be aware of bedding products; those such as sheepskin bed liners must be avoided. Lanolin, or products containing lanolin, have also been known to create an allergic reaction in this breed.

Cresteds don't mind cotton against their skin, but avoid hugging your dog when you're wearing wool. Also, try to resist biting your dog at all costs!

# CHINESE CRESTED

All breed standards are designed effectively to paint a picture in words, though each reader will almost certainly have a slightly different way of interpreting these words. When you look back to the early days and read the breed standard for the Chinese Crested, you can see that today's recognized standard is greatly detailed.

However, to fully comprehend the intricacies of a breed, reading words alone is never enough. It is just as essential for devotees to watch Chinese Cresteds being judged at shows and, if possible, to attend seminars at which the breed is discussed. This enables owners to absorb as much as possible about the breed they love so much. "Hands-on" experience, providing an opportunity to assess the structure of dogs, is always valuable, especially for those who hope ultimately to judge the breed. However familiar you are with the breed, it is always worth refreshing your memory by re-reading the standard, for it is sometimes all too easy to overlook, or perhaps conveniently forget, certain features.

A breed standard undoubtedly helps breeders to produce stock that comes as close as possible to the recognized standard and helps judges to know exactly what they are looking for in the breed. This enables a judge to make a carefully considered decision when selecting the most typical Chinese Crested present to head his line of winners.

## AMERICAN KENNEL CLUB BREED STANDARD FOR THE CHINESE CRESTED

### GENERAL APPEARANCE
A toy dog, fine-boned, elegant and graceful. The distinct varieties are born in the same litter. The Hairless with hair only on the head, tail and feet and the Powderpuff, completely covered

Head study of an adult Chinese Crested bitch, showing alert expression, smooth skin, chiselled cheeks, prominent nose and long, graceful neck.

with hair. The breed serves as a loving companion, playful and entertaining.

**SIZE, PROPORTION, SUBSTANCE**
*Size:* Ideally 11 to 13 inches. However, dogs that are slightly larger or smaller may be given full consideration. *Proportion:* Rectangular-proportioned to allow for freedom of movement. Body length from withers to base of tail is slightly longer than the height at the withers. *Substance:* Fine-boned and slender but not so refined as to appear breakable or alternatively, not a robust, heavy structure.

**HEAD**
*Expression:* Alert and intense. *Eyes:* Almond-shaped, set wide apart. Dark-colored dogs have dark-colored eyes, and lighter-colored dogs may have lighter-colored eyes. Eye rims match the coloring of the dog. *Ears:* Uncropped large and erect, placed so that the base of the ear is level with the outside corner of the eye. *Skull:* The skull is arched gently over the occiput from ear to ear. Distance from occiput to stop equal to distance from stop to tip of nose. The head is wedge-shaped viewed from above and the side. *Stop:* Slight but distinct. *Muzzle:* Cheeks taper cleanly into the muzzle. *Nose:* Dark in dark-colored dogs; may be lighter in lighter-colored dogs. Pigment is

**BETTER THAN THE AVERAGE DOG**
Even though you may never show your dog, you should still read the breed standard. The breed standard tells you more than just physical specifications such as how tall your dog should be; it also describes how he should act, how he should move and what unique qualities make him the breed that he is. You are not investing money in a pure-bred dog so that you can own a dog that "sort of looks like" the breed you're purchasing. You want a typical, handsome representative of the breed, one that all of your friends and family and people you meet out in public will recognize as the breed you've so carefully selected and researched. If the parents of your prospective puppy bear little or no resemblance to the dog described in the breed standard, you should keep searching!

solid. *Lips*: Lips are clean and tight. *Bite*: Scissors or level in both varieties. Missing teeth in the Powderpuff are to be faulted. The Hairless variety is not to be penalized for absence of full dentition.

### NECK, TOPLINE, BODY

*Neck:* Neck is lean and clean, slightly arched from the withers to the base of the skull and carried high. *Topline*: Level to slightly sloping croup. *Body:* Brisket extends to the elbow. Breastbone is not prominent. Ribs are well developed. The depth of

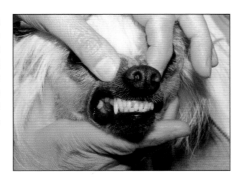

the chest tapers to a moderate tuck-up at the flanks. Light in loin. *Tail*: Tail is slender and tapers to a curve. It is long enough to reach the hock. When dog is in motion, the tail is carried gaily and may be carried slightly forward over the back. At rest the tail is down with a slight curve upward at the end resembling a sickle. In the Hairless variety, two-thirds of the end of the tail is covered by long, flowing feathering referred to as a plume. The Powderpuff variety's tail is completely covered with hair.

### FOREQUARTERS

*Angulation:* Layback of shoulders is 45 degrees to point of shoulder allowing for good reach. *Shoulders:* Clean and narrow. Elbows: Close to body. Legs: Long, slender and straight. *Pasterns:* Upright, fine and strong. Dewclaws may be removed. *Feet:* Hare foot, narrow with elongated toes. Nails are trimmed to moderate length.

### HINDQUARTERS

*Angulation*: Stifle moderately angulated. From hock joint to ground perpendicular. Dewclaws may be removed. *Feet:* Same as forequarters.

### COAT

The Hairless variety has hair on certain portions of the body: the head (called a crest), the tail

**COLOR**
Any color or combination of colors.

**GAIT**
Lively, agile and smooth without being stilted or hackneyed. Comes and goes at a trot moving in a straight line.

**TEMPERAMENT**
Gay and alert.

**Approved June 12, 1990**
**Effective April 1, 1991**

(called a plume) and the feet from the toes to the front pasterns and rear hock joints (called socks). The texture of all hair is soft and silky, flowing to any length. Placement of hair is not as important as overall type. Areas that have hair usually taper off slightly. Wherever the body is hairless, the skin is soft and smooth. Head Crest begins at the stop and tapers off between the base of the skull and the back of the neck. Hair on the ears and face is permitted on the Hairless and may be trimmed for neatness in both varieties. Tail Plume is described under Tail. The Powderpuff variety is completely covered with a double soft and silky coat. Close examination reveals long thin guard hairs over the short silky undercoat. The coat is straight, of moderate density and length. Excessively heavy, kinky or curly coat is to be penalized. Grooming is minimal, consisting of presenting a clean and neat appearance.

## FOR THE LOVE OF DOGS

Breeding involves a major financial investment, but just as important is your investment in time. You'll spend countless hours in caring for, cleaning (and cleaning up after), feeding and training the litter. Furthermore, we haven't yet mentioned the strain and health risks that delivering a litter pose to the dam. Many bitches die in puppybirth, and that is a very high price to pay. Experienced breeders, with established lines and reputations in the field, are not in the hobby for financial gain. Those "breeders" who are in it for profit are not true breeders at all, and are not reputable sources from which to buy puppies. Remember, there is nothing more to breeding dogs than the love of the dogs.

# CHINESE CRESTED

Before reaching the decision that you definitely want a Chinese Crested puppy, it is essential that you are fully clear in your mind that this is absolutely the most suitable breed for both you and your family. You should have done plenty of background "homework" on the breed, and preferably have visited a few shows at which the breed has been exhibited. This will have provided you with the opportunity to see the dogs with their breeders, owners and handlers, and you hopefully will have had a chance to see not only Hairless and Powderpuffs but also dogs of both cobby and deer type. These things are important, for you may decide that you have a preference,

> **MALE OR FEMALE?**
> Males of most dog breeds tend to be larger than their female counterparts and take longer to mature. Males also can be more dominant and territorial, especially if they are intact. Neutering before one year of age can help minimize those tendencies. Females of most breeds are often less rambunctious and easier to handle. However, individual personalities vary, so the differences are often due more to temperament than to the sex of the animal.

especially where coat is concerned. Dog shows can be good opportunities to talk with owners and breeders; most will be happy to answer your questions provided you approach them when they are not busy or awaiting a turn in the ring.

Remember that the dog you select should remain with you for the duration of its life, which is usually upwards of 13 years for a Chinese Crested, so making the right decision from the outset is of the utmost importance. No dog should be moved from one home to another simply because its

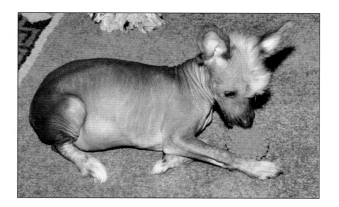

Twelve-week-old Hairless puppy, on which the signature "crest" is quite evident.

Two Hairless and a Powderpuff. Hairless-to-Hairless and Hairless-to-Powderpuff matings can produce either variety, while Powderpuff-to-Powderpuff will produce only coated pups.

owners were not considerate enough to have done sufficient background research before selecting the breed and puppy.

Always be certain that the puppy you finally select has a seemingly sound personality; it should not be overly shy or aggressive. Never take pity on an unduly shy puppy, for in doing so you will be asking for trouble in the long run. Such a dog will likely have serious problems in becoming socialized.

Puppies almost invariably

### COST OF OWNERSHIP

The purchase price of your puppy is merely the first expense in the typical dog budget. Quality dog food, veterinary care (sickness and health maintenance), dog supplies and grooming costs will add up to big bucks every year. Can you adequately afford to support a canine addition to the family?

look enchanting, but you must select one from a caring breeder who has given the puppies all the attention they deserve and who has looked after them well. They should already have been well socialized; this is likely to be apparent when you meet the litter.

The puppy you select should look well fed, but not pot-bellied, as this might indicate worms. Eyes should look bright and clear, without discharge. The nose should be moist, which is an indication of good health, but should never be runny. It goes without saying that there should certainly be no evidence of loose bowels or of parasites. The puppy you choose should have healthy-looking skin or coat, depending upon whether you have selected a Hairless or a Powderpuff.

Sex will also play a role in your decision when selecting your puppy. Do you want a male or a female? In the Chinese Crested,

Observe the adult dogs of your chosen breeder's lines as well as the pups. You want to ensure that all dogs on the premises are healthy, well cared for and temperamentally sound.

where to find a puppy and what to look for. You should inquire about breeders who enjoy a good reputation in the breed. You are looking for an established breeder with outstanding dog ethics and a strong commitment to the breed. New owners should have as many questions as they have doubts. An established breeder is indeed the one to answer your four million questions and make you comfortable with your choice of the unique Chinese Crested. An established breeder will sell you a puppy at a fair price if, and only if, the breeder determines that you are a suitable, worthy owner of his dogs. An established breeder can be relied upon for advice at

males should be larger than females, and they tend to be a little more dominant. Some say that Chinese Crested males are more loving than bitches.

Something else to consider is whether or not to take out veterinary insurance. A veterinary surgeon's bills can mount up, and you must always be certain that sufficient funds are available to give your dog any necessary veterinary attention. Keep in mind, though, that routine vaccinations will not be covered by insurance.

## SELECTING A BREEDER AND PUPPY
If you are convinced that the Chinese Crested is the ideal dog for you, it's time to learn about

### SOME DAM ATTITUDE
When selecting a puppy, be certain to meet the dam of the litter. The temperament of the dam is often predictive of the temperament of her puppies. However, dams occasionally are very protective of their young, some to the point of being testy or aggressive with visitors, whom they may view as a danger to their babies. Such attitudes are more common when the pups are very young and still nursing and should not be mistaken for actual aggressive temperament. If possible, visit the dam away from her pups to make friends with her and gain a better understanding of her true personality.

## MAKE A COMMITMENT

Dogs are most assuredly man's best friend, but they are also a lot of work. When you add a puppy to your family, you also are adding to your daily responsibilities for years to come. Dogs need more than just food, water and a place to sleep. They also require training (which can be ongoing throughout the lifetime of the dog), activity to keep them physically and mentally fit and hands-on attention every day, plus grooming and health care. Your life as you now know it may well disappear! Are you prepared for such drastic changes?

quality Chinese Cresteds, as can the American Chinese Crested Club or a local all-breed club or Chinese Crested club.

Once you have contacted and met a breeder or two and made your choice about which breeder is best suited to your needs, it's time to visit the litter. Keep in mind that it will take some time to locate a Chinese Crested litter and, once you do, you will probably have to put your name on a waiting list for a puppy. Sometimes new owners have to wait as long as two years for a puppy. If you are really committed to the breeder whom you've selected, then you will wait (and hope for an early arrival!). If not, you may have to resort to your second- or third-choice breeder. Don't be too anxious, however. If the breeder doesn't have a waiting list, or any customers, there is probably a

any reasonable time during the course of your dog's life. Many breeders will accept a puppy back with little or no penalty to you, should you decide that this is not the right dog for you.

Choosing a breeder is an important first step in dog ownership. When choosing a breeder, reputation is much more important than convenience of location. Fortunately, the majority of Chinese Crested breeders are devoted to the breed and its well-being. The American Kennel Club is able to recommend breeders of

The whole family should take part in the selection process, from visiting the breeder to picking the perfect pup.

good reason. It's no different from visiting an eating or drinking place with no clientele. The better bars and restaurants often have waiting lists—and it's usually worth the wait. Besides, isn't a puppy more important than a meal?

### PEDIGREE VS. REGISTRATION CERTIFICATE

Too often new owners are confused between these two important documents. Your puppy's pedigree, essentially a family tree, is a written record of a dog's genealogy of three generations or more. The pedigree will show you the names as well as performance titles of all dogs in your pup's background. Your breeder must provide you with a registration application, with his part properly filled out. You must complete the application and send it to the AKC with the proper fee. Every puppy must come from a litter that has been AKC-registered by the breeder, born in the US and from a sire and dam that are also registered with the AKC.

The seller must provide you with complete records to identify the puppy. The AKC requires that the seller provide the buyer with the following: breed; sex, color and markings; date of birth; litter number (when available); names and registration numbers of the parents; breeder's name; and date sold or delivered.

Since you are likely to be choosing a Chinese Crested as a pet dog and not a show dog, you simply should select a pup that is friendly, attractive and healthy. Chinese Crested litters average about five puppies, so selection is somewhat limited once you have located a desirable litter.

Breeders commonly allow visitors to see their litters by around the fifth or sixth week, and puppies leave for their new homes around the tenth to twelfth week. Breeders who permit their puppies to leave early are more interested in your money than in their puppies' well-being. Puppies need to learn the rules of the pack from their dams, and most dams continue teaching the pups manners and dos and don'ts until around the eighth week. Breeders spend significant amounts of time with the Chinese Crested toddlers so that the pups are able to interact with the "other species," i.e. humans. Given the long history that dogs and humans have, bonding between the two species is natural but must be nurtured. A well-bred, well-socialized Chinese Crested pup

## GETTING ACQUAINTED

When visiting a litter, ask the breeder for suggestions on how best to interact with the puppies. If possible, get right into the middle of the pack and sit down with them. Observe which pups climb into your lap and which ones shy away. Toss a toy for them to chase and bring back to you. It's easy to fall in love with the puppy who picks you, but keep your future objectives in mind before you make your final decision.

wants nothing more than to be near you and please you.

## A COMMITTED NEW OWNER

By now you should understand what makes the Chinese Crested a most unique and special dog, one that may fit nicely into your family and lifestyle. If you have researched breeders, you should be able to recognize a knowledgeable and responsible Chinese Crested breeder who cares not only about his pups but also about what kind of owner you will be. If you have completed the final step in your new journey, you have found a litter, or possibly two, of quality Chinese Crested pups.

A visit with the puppies and their breeder should be an education in itself. Breed research, breeder selection and puppy visitation are very important aspects of finding the puppy of your dreams. Beyond that, these things also lay the foundation for a successful future with your pup. Puppy personalities within each litter vary, from the shy and easygoing puppy to the one who is dominant and assertive, with most pups falling somewhere in between. By spending time with the puppies you will be able to recognize certain behaviors and what these behaviors indicate about each pup's temperament. Which type of pup will complement your family dynamics is best determined by

## A SHOW PUPPY

If you plan to show your puppy, you must first deal with a reputable breeder who shows his dogs and has had some success in the conformation ring. The puppy's pedigree should include one or more champions in the first and second generation. You should be familiar with the breed and breed standard so you can know what qualities to look for in your puppy. The breeder's observations and recommendations also are invaluable aids in selecting your future champion. If you consider an older puppy, be sure that the puppy has been properly socialized with people and not isolated in a kennel without substantial daily human contact.

observing the puppies in action within their "pack." Your breeder's expertise and recommendations are also valuable. Although you may fall in love with a bold and brassy male, the breeder may suggest that another pup would be best for you. The breeder's experience in rearing Chinese Crested pups and matching their temperaments with appropriate humans offers the best assurance that your pup will meet your needs and expectations. The type of puppy that you select is just as important as your decision that the Chinese Crested is the breed for you.

The decision to live with a Chinese Crested is a serious commitment and not one to be taken lightly. This puppy is a living sentient being that will be dependent on you for basic survival for his entire life. Beyond the basics of survival—food, water, shelter and protection—he needs much, much more. The new pup needs love, nurturing and a proper canine education to mold him into a responsible, well-behaved canine citizen. Your Chinese Crested's health and good manners will need consistent monitoring and regular "tune-ups," so your job as a responsible dog owner will be ongoing throughout every stage of his life. If you are not prepared to accept these responsibilities and commit to them for the next decade, likely longer, then you are not prepared to own a dog of any breed.

Although the responsibilities of owning a dog may at times tax your patience, the joy of living with your Chinese Crested far outweighs the workload, and a well-mannered adult dog is worth your time and effort. Before your very eyes, your new charge will grow up to be your most loyal friend, devoted to you unconditionally.

**FIRST CAR RIDE**

The ride to your home from the breeder will no doubt be your puppy's first automobile experience, and you should make every effort to keep him comfortable and secure. Bring a large towel or small blanket for the puppy to lie on during the trip and an extra towel in case the pup gets carsick or has a potty accident. It's best to have another person with you to hold the puppy in his lap. Most puppies will fall fast asleep from the rolling motion of the car. If the ride is lengthy, you may have to stop so that the puppy can relieve himself, so be sure to bring a leash and collar for those stops. Avoid rest areas for potty trips, since those are frequented by many dogs, who may carry parasites or disease. It's better to stop at grassy areas near gas stations or shopping centers to prevent unhealthy exposure for your pup.

## YOUR CHINESE CRESTED SHOPPING LIST

Just as expectant parents prepare a nursery for their baby, so should you ready your home for the arrival of your Chinese Crested pup. If you have the necessary puppy supplies purchased and in place before he comes home, it will ease the puppy's transition from the warmth and familiarity of his mom and littermates to the brand-new environment of his new home and human family. You will be too busy to stock up and prepare your house after your pup comes home, that's for sure! Imagine how a pup must feel upon being transported to a strange new place. It's up to you to comfort him and to let your little pup know that he is going to be happy with you.

*Your Crested puppy should be approachable, if a little reserved, and ready to meet new friends.*

### FOOD AND WATER BOWLS

Your puppy will need separate bowls for his food and water.

Alert and inquisitive, Chinese Crested pups can get into trouble unless they are supervised properly.

Stainless steel pans are generally preferred over plastic bowls since they sterilize better and pups are less inclined to chew on the metal. Heavy-duty ceramic bowls are popular, but consider how often you will have to pick up those heavy bowls. Buy adult-sized pans, as your puppy will grow into them before you know it.

### THE DOG CRATE

If you think that crates are tools of punishment and confinement for when a dog has misbehaved, think again. Most breeders and almost all trainers recommend a crate as the preferred house-training aid as well as for all-around puppy training and safety. Because dogs are natural den creatures that prefer cave-like environments, the benefits of crate use are many. The crate provides the puppy with his very own "safe house," a cozy place to sleep, take a break or seek comfort with a favorite toy; a travel aid to house your dog when on the road, at motels or at the vet's office; a training aid to help teach your puppy proper toileting habits; a place of solitude when non-dog people happen to drop by and don't want a lively puppy—or even a well-behaved adult dog—saying hello or begging for attention.

Crates come in several types, although the wire crate and the

### CRATE EXPECTATIONS

To make the crate more inviting to your puppy, you can offer his first meal or two inside the crate, always keeping the crate door open so that he does not feel confined. Keep a favorite toy or two in the crate for him to play with while inside. You can also cover the crate at night with a lightweight sheet to make it more den-like and remove the stimuli of household activity. Never put him into his crate as punishment or as you are scolding him, since he will then associate his crate with negative situations and avoid going there.

fiberglass airline-type crate are the most popular. Both are safe and your puppy will adjust to either one, so the choice is up to you. The wire crates offer better visibility for the pup as well as better ventilation. Many of the wire crates easily collapse into suitcase-size carriers. The fiberglass crates, similar to those used by the airlines for animal transport, are sturdier and more den-like. However, the fiberglass crates do not collapse and are less ventilated than a wire crate, which can be problematic in hot weather. Some of the newer crates are made of heavy plastic mesh; they are very lightweight and fold up into slim-line suitcases. However, a mesh crate might not be suitable for a pup with manic chewing habits.

Don't bother with a puppy-

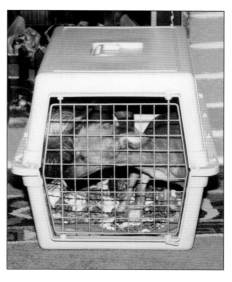

Your puppy's crate will serve as a place of retreat... a home within his new home.

sized crate. Although your Chinese Crested will be a wee fellow when you bring him home, he will grow up in the blink of an eye and your puppy crate will be useless. Purchase a crate that will accommodate an adult Chinese Crested. He will stand about a foot tall when full grown, so a small- to medium-sized crate will fit him nicely.

### BEDDING AND CRATE PADS

Your puppy will enjoy some type of soft bedding in his "room" (the crate), something he can snuggle into to feel cozy and secure. Old towels or blankets are good choices for a young pup, since he may (and probably will) have a toileting accident or two in the crate or decide to chew on the bedding material. Once he is fully

---

### WHAT SIZE IS THE RIGHT SIZE?

When purchasing a crate, buy one that will fit an adult-size dog. Puppy crates are poor investments, since puppies quickly outgrow them. The crate should accommodate an adult dog in a standing position so that he has room to stand up, turn around and lie down comfortably. A larger crate is fine but not necessary for the dog's comfort, as most of his crate time will be spent lying down and napping.

Your local pet shop will have a variety of crates from which you can choose a sturdy model of a suitable size for your Chinese Crested.

trained and out of the early chewing stage, you can replace the puppy bedding with a permanent crate pad if you prefer. Crate pads and other dog beds run the gamut from inexpensive to high-end doggie-designer styles, but don't splurge on the good stuff until you are sure that your puppy is reliable and won't tear it up or make a mess on it.

### Puppy Toys

Just as infants and older children require objects to stimulate their minds and bodies, puppies need toys to entertain their curious brains, wiggly paws and achy teeth. A fun array of safe doggie toys will help satisfy your puppy's chewing instincts and distract him from gnawing on the leg of your antique chair or your new leather sofa. Most puppy toys are cute and look as if they would be a lot of fun, but not all are necessarily safe or good for your puppy, so use caution when you go puppy-toy shopping.

Although Chinese Cresteds are not known to be voracious chewers like many other dogs, they still love to chew. The best "chewcifiers" are nylon and hard rubber bones which are safe to gnaw on and come in sizes appropriate for all age groups and breeds. Be especially careful of natural bones, which can splinter or develop dangerous sharp edges; pups can easily swallow or choke on those bone splinters. Veterinarians often tell of surgical nightmares involving bits of splintered bone, because in addition to the danger of choking, the sharp pieces can damage the intestinal tract.

Similarly, rawhide chews,

### ROCK-A-BYE BEDDING
The wide assortment of dog beds today can make your choice quite difficult, as there are many adorable novelty beds in fun styles and prints. It's wise to wait until your puppy has outgrown the chewing stage before providing him with a dog bed, since he might make confetti out of it. Your puppy will be happy with an old towel or blanket in his crate until he is old enough to resist the temptation to chew up his bed. For a dog of any age, a bed with a washable cover is always a wise choice.

## TEETHING TIME

All puppies chew. It's normal canine behavior. Chewing just plain feels good to a puppy, especially during the three- to five-month teething period when the adult teeth are breaking through the gums. Rather than attempting to eliminate such a strong natural chewing instinct, you will be more successful if you redirect it and teach your puppy what he may or may not chew. Correct inappropriate chewing with a sharp "No!" and offer him a chew toy, praising him when he takes it. Don't become discouraged. Chewing usually decreases after the adult teeth have come in.

while a favorite of most dogs and puppies, can be equally dangerous. Pieces of rawhide are easily swallowed after they get all gummy from chewing, and dogs have been known to choke on large pieces of ingested rawhide. Rawhide chews should be offered only when you can supervise the puppy.

Soft woolly toys are special puppy favorites. They come in a wide variety of cute shapes and sizes; some look like little stuffed animals. Puppies love to shake them up and toss them about, or simply carry them around. Be careful of fuzzy toys that have button eyes or noses that your pup could chew off and swallow, and make sure that he does not

A remarkable gallery of Chinese Cresteds in their crates. Show dogs are always crate trained.

## TOYS 'R SAFE

The vast array of tantalizing puppy toys is staggering. Stroll through any pet shop or pet-supply outlet and you will see that the choices can be overwhelming. However, not all dog toys are safe or sensible. Most very young puppies enjoy soft woolly toys that they can snuggle with and carry around. (You know they have outgrown them when they shred them up!) Avoid toys that have buttons, tabs or other enhancements that can be chewed off and swallowed. Soft toys that squeak are fun, but make sure your puppy does not disembowel the toy and remove (and swallow) the squeaker. Toys that rattle or make noise can excite a puppy, but they present the same danger as the squeaky kind and so require supervision. Hard rubber toys that bounce can also entertain a pup, but make sure that the toy is too big for your pup to swallow.

disembowel a squeaky toy to remove the squeaker! Braided rope toys are similar in that they are fun to chew and toss around, but they shred easily and the strings are easy to swallow. The strings are not digestible and, if the puppy doesn't pass them in his stool, he could end up at the vet's office. As with rawhides, your puppy should be closely monitored with rope toys.

If you believe that your pup has ingested one of these forbidden objects, check his stools for the next couple of days to see if he passes them when he defecates. At the same time, also watch for signs of intestinal distress. A call to your veterinarian might be in order to get his advice and be on the safe side.

An all-time favorite toy for puppies (young and old!) is the empty gallon milk jug. Hard plastic juice containers—46 ounces or more—are also excellent. Such containers make lots of noise when they are batted about, and puppies go crazy with delight as they play with them. However, they don't often last very long, so be sure to remove and replace them when they get chewed up on the ends.

A word of caution about homemade toys: be careful with your choices of non-traditional play objects. Never use old shoes or socks, since a puppy cannot

distinguish between the old ones on which he's allowed to chew and the new ones in your closet that are strictly off limits. That principle applies to anything that resembles something that you don't want your puppy to chew up.

## DIGGING OUT

Some dogs love to dig. Others wouldn't think of it. Digging is considered "self-rewarding behavior" because it's fun! Of all the digging solutions offered by the experts, most are only marginally successful and none is guaranteed to work. The best cure is prevention, which means removing the dog from the offending site when he digs as well as distracting him when you catch him digging so that he turns his attentions elsewhere. That means that you have to supervise your dog's yard time. An unsupervised digger can create havoc with your landscaping or, worse, run away!

### COLLARS

A lightweight nylon collar is the best choice for a very young pup. Quick-clip collars are easy to put on and remove, and they can be adjusted as the puppy grows. Introduce him to his collar as soon as he comes home to get him accustomed to wearing it. He'll get used to it quickly and won't mind a bit. Make sure that it is snug enough that it won't slip off, yet loose enough to be comfortable for the pup. You should be able to slip two fingers between the collar and his neck. Check the collar often, as puppies grow in spurts, and his collar can become too tight almost overnight. Choke collars are for training purposes only and should never be used on a puppy under four or five months old.

If not given proper chew toys, your Crested will find things on which to chew, which could be dangerous to his teeth and his health.

Accustom your pup to his lead and collar at an early age. Only a light nylon lead and collar are needed for a Chinese Crested.

# Leash Life

Dogs love leashes! Believe it or not, most dogs dance for joy every time their owners pick up their leashes. The leash means that the dog is going for a walk—and there are few things more exciting than that! Here are some of the kinds of leashes that are commercially available.

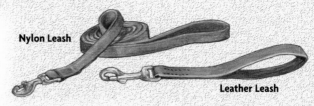

**Nylon Leash**

**Leather Leash**

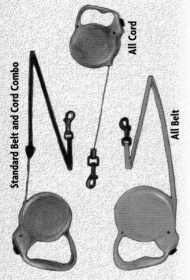

**Standard Belt and Cord Combo**

**All Cord**

**All Belt**

**Retractable Leashes**

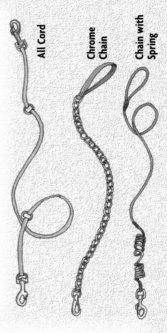

**All Cord**

**Chrome Chain**

**Chain with Spring**

**Traditional Leash:** Made of cotton, nylon or leather, these leashes are usually about 6 feet in length. A quality-made leather leash is softer on the hands than a nylon one. Durable woven cotton is a popular option. Lengths can vary up to about 48 feet, designed for different uses.

**Chain Leash:** Usually a metal chain leash with a plastic handle. This is not the best choice for most breeds, as it is heavier than other leashes and difficult to manage.

**Retractable Leash:** A long nylon cord is housed in a plastic device for extending and retracting. This leash, also known as a flexible leash, is ideal for taking trained dogs for long walks in open areas, although it is not always suitable for large, powerful breeds. Different lengths and sizes are available, so check that you purchase one appropriate for your dog's weight.

**Elastic Leash:** A nylon leash with an elastic extension. This is useful for well-trained dogs, especially in conjunction with a head halter.

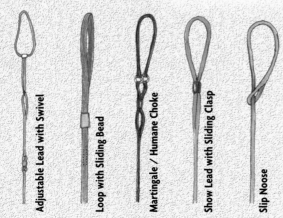

**Adjustable Lead with Swivel**

**Loop with Sliding Bead**

**Martingale / Humane Choke**

**Show Lead with Sliding Clasp**

**Slip Noose**

**A Variety of Collar-and-Leash-in-One Products**

Avoid leashes that are completely elastic, as they afford minimal control to the handler.

**Adjustable Leash:** This has two snaps, one on each end, and several metal rings. It is handy if you need to tether your dog temporarily, but is never to be used with a choke collar.

**Tab Leash:** A short leash (4 to 6 inches long) that attaches to your dog's collar. This device serves like a handle, in case you have to grab your dog while he's exercising off lead. It's ideal for "half-trained" dogs or dogs that listen only half of the time.

**Slip Leash:** Essentially a leash with a collar built in, similar to what a dog-show handler uses to show a dog. This British-style collar has a ring on the end so that you can form a slip collar. Useful if you have to catch your own runaway dog or a stray.

# COLLARING OUR CANINES

The standard flat collar with a buckle or a snap, in leather, nylon or cotton, is widely regarded as the everyday all-purpose collar. If the collar fits correctly, you should be able to fit two fingers between the collar and the dog's neck.

**Leather Buckle Collars**

**Limited-Slip Collar**

The martingale, Greyhound or limited-slip collar is preferred by many dog owners and trainers. It is fixed with an extra loop that tightens when pressure is applied to the leash. The martingale collar gets tighter but does not "choke" the dog. The limited-slip collar should only be used for walking and training, not for free play or interaction with another dog. These types of collar should never be left on the dog, as the extra loop can lead to accidents.

Choke collars, usually made of stainless steel, are made for training purposes but are not recommended for small dogs or heavily coated breeds. The chains can injure small dogs or damage long/abundant coats. Thin nylon choke leads are commonly used on show dogs while in the ring, though they are not practical for everyday use.

The harness, with two or three straps that attach over the dog's shoulders and around his torso, is a humane and safe alternative to the conventional collar. By and large, a well-made harness is virtually escape-proof. Harnesses are available in nylon and mesh and can be outfitted on most dogs, ranging in chest girths of 10 to 30 inches.

**Snap Bolt Choke Collar**

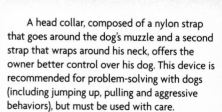

**Harness**

**Nylon Collar**

**Quick-Click Closure**

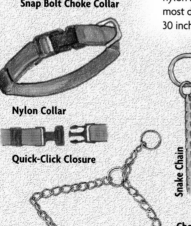

**Snake Chain**

**Chrome Steel**

**Fur-Saver**

**Choke Chain Collars**

A head collar, composed of a nylon strap that goes around the dog's muzzle and a second strap that wraps around his neck, offers the owner better control over his dog. This device is recommended for problem-solving with dogs (including jumping up, pulling and aggressive behaviors), but must be used with care.

A training halter, including a flat collar and two straps, made of nylon and webbing, is designed for walking. There are several on the market; some are more difficult to put on the dog than others. The halter harness, with two small slip rings at each end, is recommended for ease of use.

Mischievous and curious, Crested puppies love interactive games and fun toys.

## LEASHES

A 6-foot nylon lead is an excellent choice for a young puppy. It is lightweight and not as tempting to chew as a leather lead. You can switch to a 6-foot leather lead after your pup has grown and is used to walking politely on a lead. For initial puppy walks and house-training purposes, you should invest in a shorter lead so that you have more control over the puppy. At first, you don't want him wandering too far away from you, and when taking him out for toileting you will want to keep him in the specific area chosen for his potty spot.

Once the puppy is heel trained with a traditional leash, you can consider purchasing a retractable lead. A retractable lead is excellent for walking adult dogs that are already leash-wise. This type of lead allows the dog to roam farther away from you and explore a wider area when out walking, and also retracts when you need to keep him close to you.

## HOME SAFETY FOR YOUR PUPPY

The importance of puppy-proofing cannot be overstated. In addition to making your house comfortable for your Chinese Crested's arrival, you also must make sure that your house is safe for your puppy before you bring him home. There are countless hazards in the owner's personal living environment that a pup can sniff, chew, swallow or destroy. Many are obvious; others are not. Do a thorough advance house check to remove or rearrange those things that could hurt your puppy, keeping any potentially dangerous items out of areas to which he will have access.

Electrical cords are especially dangerous, since puppies view them as irresistible chew toys. Unplug and remove all exposed cords or fasten them beneath a baseboard where the puppy

### TOXIC PLANTS

Plants are natural puppy magnets, but many can be harmful, even fatal, if ingested by a puppy or adult dog. Scout your yard and home interior and remove any plants, bushes or flowers that could be even mildly dangerous. It could save your puppy's life. You can obtain a complete list of toxic plants from your veterinarian, at the public library or by looking online.

cannot reach them. Veterinarians and firefighters can tell you horror stories about electrical burns and house fires that resulted from puppy-chewed electrical cords. Consider this a most serious precaution for your puppy and the rest of your family.

Scout your home for tiny objects that might be seen at a pup's eye level. Keep medication bottles and cleaning supplies well out of reach, and do the same with waste baskets and other trash containers. It goes without saying that you should not use rodent poison or other toxic chemicals in any puppy area and that you must keep such containers safely locked up. You will be amazed at how many places a curious puppy can discover!

Once your house has cleared inspection, check your yard. A sturdy fence, well embedded into the ground, will give your dog a safe place to play and potty. Although Chinese Cresteds are not known to be climbers or fence jumpers, they are still athletic dogs, so a 5- to 6-foot-high fence should be adequate to contain an agile youngster or adult. Check the fence periodically for necessary repairs. If there is a weak link or space to squeeze through, you can be sure a determined Chinese Crested will discover it.

The garage and shed can be hazardous places for a pup, as things like fertilizers, chemicals and tools are usually kept there. It's best to keep these areas off limits to the pup. Antifreeze is especially dangerous to dogs, as they find the taste appealing and it takes only a few licks from the

Your watchful eyes are necessary for your pup's safety and to keep him from sticking his nose into trouble!

Your Crested's veterinarian will soon become his *other* best friend.

driveway to kill a dog, puppy or adult.

**VISITING THE VETERINARIAN**
A good veterinarian is your Chinese Crested puppy's best health insurance policy. If you do not already have a vet, ask friends and experienced dog people in your area for recommendations so that you can select a vet before you bring your Chinese Crested puppy home. Also arrange for your puppy's first veterinary examination beforehand, since many vets have two- and three-week waiting periods and your puppy should visit the vet within a day or so of coming home.

It's important to make sure your puppy's first visit to the vet is a pleasant and positive one.

The vet should take great care to befriend the pup and handle him gently to make their first meeting a positive experience. The vet will give the pup a thorough physical examination and set up a schedule for vaccinations and other necessary wellness visits. Be sure to show your vet any health and inoculation records, which you should have received from your breeder. Your vet is a great source of canine health information, so be sure to ask questions and take notes. Creating a health journal for your puppy will make a handy reference for his wellness and any future health problems that may arise.

**ASK THE VET**
Help your vet help you to become a well-informed dog owner. Don't be shy about becoming involved in your puppy's veterinary care by asking questions and gaining as much knowledge as you can. For starters, ask what shots your puppy is getting and what diseases they prevent, and discuss with your vet the safest way to vaccinate. Find out what is involved in your dog's annual wellness visits. If you plan to spay or neuter, discuss the best age at which to have this done. Start out on the right "paw" with your puppy's vet and develop good communication with him, as he will care for your dog's health throughout the dog's life.

## PUPPY SHOTS

Puppies are born with natural antibodies that protect them from most canine diseases. They receive more antibodies from the colostrum in their mother's milk. These immunities wear off, however, and must be replaced through a series of vaccines. Puppy shots are given at 3- to 4-week intervals starting at 6 to 8 weeks of age through 16 to 20 weeks of age. Booster shots are given after one year of age, and every one to three years thereafter.

## MEETING THE FAMILY

Your Chinese Crested's homecoming is an exciting time for all members of the family, and it's only natural that everyone will be eager to meet him, pet him and play with him. However, for the puppy's sake, it's best to make these initial family meetings as uneventful as possible so that the pup is not overwhelmed with too much too soon. Remember, he has just left his dam and his littermates and is away from the breeder's home for the first time. Despite his fuzzy wagging tail, he is still apprehensive and wondering where he is and who all these strange humans are. It's best to let him explore on his own and meet the family members as he feels comfortable. Let him investigate all the new smells, sights and sounds at his own pace. Children should be especially careful to not get overly excited, use loud voices or hug the pup too tightly. Be calm, gentle and affectionate, and be ready to comfort him if he appears frightened or uneasy.

Be sure to show your puppy his new crate during this first day home. Toss a treat or two inside the crate; if he associates the crate with food, he will associate the crate with good things. If he is comfortable with the crate, you can offer him his first meal inside it. Leave the door ajar so he can wander in and out as he chooses.

Discuss your Crested puppy's inoculation schedule with your veterinarian. Make this one of your top priorities as a new puppy owner.

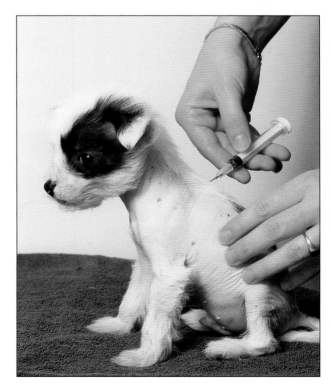

## FIRST NIGHT IN HIS NEW HOME

So much has happened in your Chinese Crested puppy's first day away from the breeder. He's had his first car ride to his new home. He's met his new human family and perhaps the other family pets. He has explored his new house and yard, at least those places where he is to be allowed during his first weeks at home. He may have visited his new veterinarian. He has eaten his first meal or two away from his dam and litter-mates. Surely that's enough to tire out a ten-week-old Chinese Crested pup...or so you hope!

It's bedtime. During the day, the pup investigated his crate, which is his new den and sleeping space, so it is not entirely strange to him. Line the crate with a soft towel or blanket that he can snuggle into and gently place him into the crate for the night. Some breeders send home a piece of bedding from where the pup slept with his littermates, and those familiar scents are a great comfort for the puppy on his first night without his siblings.

He will probably whine or cry. The puppy is objecting to the confinement and the fact that he is alone for the first time. This can be a stressful time for you as well as for the pup. It's important that you remain strong and don't let the puppy out of his crate to comfort him. He will fall asleep eventually. If you release him, the puppy will learn that crying means "out" and will continue that habit. You are laying the groundwork for future habits. Some breeders find that soft music can soothe a crying pup and help him get to sleep.

### THE CRITICAL SOCIALIZATION PERIOD

Canine research has shown that a puppy's 8th through 16th week is the most critical learning period of his life. This is when the puppy "learns to learn," a time when he needs positive experiences to build confidence and stability. Puppies who are not exposed to different people and situations outside the home during this period can grow up to be fearful and sometimes aggressive. This is also the best time for puppy lessons, since he has not yet acquired any bad habits that could undermine his ability to learn.

## SOCIALIZING YOUR PUPPY

The next 20 weeks of your Chinese Crested puppy's life are

the most important of his entire lifetime. A properly socialized puppy will grow up to be a confident and stable adult who will be a pleasure to live with and a welcome addition to the neighborhood.

The importance of socialization cannot be overemphasized. Research on canine behavior has proven that puppies who are not exposed to new sights, sounds, people and animals during their first 20 weeks of life will grow up to be timid and fearful, even aggressive, and unable to flourish outside of their home environment.

Socializing your puppy is not difficult and, in fact, will be a fun time for you both. Lead training goes hand in hand with socialization, so your puppy will be learning how to walk on a lead at

the same time that he's meeting the neighborhood. Because the Chinese Crested is such a fabulous breed, your puppy will enjoy being "the new kid on the block." Take him for short walks, to the park and to other dog-friendly places where he will encounter new people, especially children. Puppies automatically recognize children as "little people" and are drawn to play with them. Just make sure that you supervise these meetings and that the children do not get too rough or encourage him to play too hard. An overzealous pup can often nip too hard, frightening the child and in turn making the puppy overly excited. A bad experience in puppyhood can impact a dog for life, so a pup that has a negative experience with a child may grow up to be shy or even aggressive around children.

Take your puppy along on your daily errands. Puppies are natural "people magnets," and most people who see your pup

**Pups should be socialized with people, including children, and also with other dogs during their early life.**

### THE FAMILY TREE

Your puppy's pedigree is his family tree. Just as a child may resemble his parents and grandparents, so too will a puppy reflect the qualities, good and bad, of his ancestors, especially those in the first two generations. Therefore it's important to know as much as possible about a puppy's immediate relatives. Reputable and experienced breeders should be able to explain the pedigree and why they chose to breed from the particular dogs they used.

will want to pet him. All of these encounters will help to mold him into a confident adult dog. Likewise, you will soon feel like a confident, responsible dog owner, rightly proud of your handsome Chinese Crested.

Be especially careful of your puppy's encounters and experiences during the eight-to-ten-week-old period, which is also called the "fear period." This is a serious imprinting period, and all contact during this time should be gentle and positive. A frightening or negative event could leave a permanent impression that could affect his future behavior if a similar situation arises.

Also make sure that your puppy has received his first and second rounds of vaccinations before you expose him to other dogs or bring him to places that other dogs may frequent. Avoid dog parks and other strange-dog areas until your vet assures you that your puppy is fully immunized and resistant to the diseases that can be passed between canines. Discuss socialization with your breeder, as some breeders recommend socializing the puppy even before he has received all of his inoculations, depending on how outgoing the puppy may be.

**LEADER OF THE PUPPY'S PACK**
Like other canines, your puppy needs an authority figure, someone he can look up to and regard as the leader of his "pack." His first pack leader was his dam, who taught him to be polite and not chew too hard on her ears or nip at her muzzle. He learned those same lessons from his littermates. If he played too rough, they cried in pain and stopped the game, which sent an important message to the rowdy puppy.

As puppies play together, they are also struggling to determine who will be the boss. Being pack animals, dogs need someone to be in charge. If a litter of puppies remained together beyond puppyhood, one of the pups would emerge as the strongest one, the one who calls the shots.

Once your puppy leaves the pack, he will look intuitively for a new leader. If he does not recognize you as that leader, he will try to assume that position for himself. Of course, it is hard to imagine your adorable Chinese Crested puppy trying to be in charge when he is so small and seemingly helpless. You must remember that these are natural canine instincts. Do not cave in and allow your pup to get the upper "paw"!

Just as socialization is so important during these first 20 weeks, so too is your puppy's early education. He was born without any bad habits. He does not know what is good or bad behavior. If he does things like nipping and digging, it's because he is having fun and doesn't know that humans consider these things as "bad." It's your job to teach him proper puppy manners, and this is the best time to accomplish that...before he has developed bad habits, since it is much more difficult to "unlearn" or correct unacceptable learned behavior than to teach good behavior from the start.

Make sure that all members of the family understand the importance of being consistent when training their new puppy. If you tell the puppy to stay off the sofa and your daughter allows him to cuddle on the couch to watch her favorite television show, your pup will be confused about what he is and is not allowed to do. Have a family conference before your pup comes home so that everyone understands the basic principles of puppy training and the rules you have set forth for the pup, and agrees to follow them.

The old saying that "an ounce of prevention is worth a pound of cure" is especially true when it comes to puppies. It is much easier to prevent inappropriate behavior than it is to change it. It's also easier and less stressful for the pup, since it will keep discipline to a minimum and create a more positive learning environment for him. That, in turn, will also be easier on you.

## PREVENTING PUPPY PROBLEMS

Here are a few commonsense tips to keep your belongings safe and your puppy out of trouble:

- Keep your closet doors closed and your shoes, socks and other apparel off the floor so your puppy can't get at them.
- Keep a secure lid on the trash container or put the trash where your puppy can't dig into it. He can't damage what he can't reach!
- Supervise your puppy at all times to make sure he is not getting into mischief. If he starts to chew the corner of the rug,

If you don't want your Chinese Crested to be allowed onto the furniture as an adult, make sure that you make that clear to him while he's a pup.

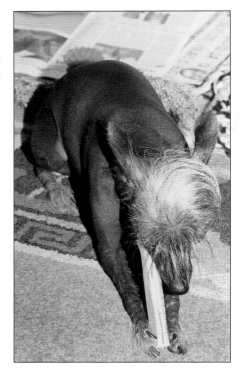

A safe chew toy will keep your pup occupied and his interests diverted from causing puppy mischief.

acceptable. That won't happen overnight and at times puppy teeth will test your patience. However, if you allow nipping and chewing to continue, just think about the damage that a mature Chinese Crested can do with a full set of adult teeth.

Whenever your puppy nips your hand or fingers, cry out "Ouch!" in a loud voice, which should startle your puppy and stop him from nipping, even if only for a moment. Immediately distract him by offering a small treat or an appropriate toy for him to chew instead (which means having chew toys and puppy treats handy or in your pockets at all times). Praise him when he takes the toy and tell him what a good fellow he is. Praise is just as or even more important in puppy training as discipline and correction.

Puppies also tend to nip at children more often than adults, since they perceive little ones to be more vulnerable and more similar to their littermates. Teach your children appropriate responses to nipping behavior. If they are unable to handle it themselves, you may have to intervene. Puppy nips can be quite painful and a child's frightened reaction will only encourage a puppy to nip harder, which is a natural canine response. As with all other puppy situations, interaction between your Chinese

you can distract him instantly by tossing a toy for him to fetch. You also will be able to whisk him outside when you notice that he is about to piddle on the carpet. If you can't see your puppy, you can't teach or correct his behavior.

### CHEWING AND NIPPING
Nipping at fingers and toes is normal puppy behavior. Chewing is also the way that puppies investigate their surroundings. However, you will have to teach your puppy that chewing anything other than his toys is not

Crested puppy and children should be supervised.

Chewing on objects, not just family members' fingers and ankles, is also normal canine behavior that can be especially tedious (for the owner, not the pup) during the teething period when the puppy's adult teeth are coming in. At this stage, chewing just plain feels good. Furniture legs and cabinet corners are common puppy favorites. Shoes and other personal items also taste pretty good to a pup.

The best solution is, once again, prevention. If you value something, keep it tucked away and out of reach. You can't hide your dining-room table in a closet, but you can try to deflect the chewing by applying a bitter product made just to deter dogs from chewing. Available in a spray or cream, this substance is vile-tasting, although safe for dogs, and most puppies will avoid the forbidden object after one tiny

### BE CONSISTENT

Consistency is a key element, in fact is absolutely necessary, to a puppy's learning environment. A behavior (such as chewing, jumping up or climbing onto the furniture) cannot be forbidden one day and then allowed the next. That will only confuse the pup, and he will not understand what he is supposed to do. Just one or two episodes of allowing an undesirable behavior to "slide" will imprint that behavior on a puppy's brain and make that behavior more difficult to erase or change.

taste. You also can apply the product to your leather leash if the puppy tries to chew on his lead during leash-training sessions.

Keep a ready supply of safe chews handy to offer your Chinese Crested as a distraction when he starts to chew on something that's a "no-no." Remember, at this tender age, he does not yet know what is permitted or forbidden, so you have to be "on call" every minute he's awake and on the prowl.

You may lose a treasure or two during puppy's growing-up period, and the furniture could sustain a nasty nick or two. These can be trying times, so be prepared for those inevitable accidents and comfort yourself in knowing that this too shall pass.

*If you own more than one Chinese Crested, you should be impartial in rewarding and disciplining them; Cresteds are sensitive enough to detect favoritism.*

### JUMPING UP

Although Chinese Crested pups are not known to be notorious jumpers, they are still puppies after all, and puppies jump up...on you, your guests, your counters and your furniture. Just another normal part of growing up, and one you need to meet head-on before it becomes an ingrained habit.

The key to jump correction is consistency. You cannot correct your Chinese Crested for jumping

**HAPPY PUPPIES COME RUNNING**
Never call your puppy (or adult dog) to come to you and then scold him or discipline him when he gets there. He will make a natural association between coming to you and being scolded, and he will think he was a bad dog for coming to you. He will then be reluctant to come whenever he is called. Always praise your puppy every time he comes to you.

Highly intelligent, Chinese Cresteds also are responsive and trainable.

up on you today, then allow it to happen tomorrow by greeting him with hugs and kisses. As you have learned by now, consistency is critical to all puppy lessons.

For starters, try turning your back as soon as the puppy jumps. Jumping up is a means of gaining your attention and, if the pup can't see your face, he may get discouraged and learn that he loses eye contact with his beloved master when he jumps up.

Leash corrections also work, and most puppies respond well to a leash tug if they jump. Grasp the leash close to the puppy's collar and give a quick tug downward, using the command "Off." Do not use the word "Down," since "Down" is used to teach the puppy to lie down, which is a separate action that he will learn during his education in the basic commands. As soon as the puppy has backed off, tell him to sit and immediately praise him for doing so. This will take many repetitions and won't be accomplished quickly, so don't get discouraged or give up; you must be even more persistent than your puppy.

A second method used for jump correction is the spritzer bottle. Fill a spray bottle with water mixed with a bit of lemon juice or vinegar. As soon as puppy jumps, command him "Off" and spritz him with the water mixture. Of course, that means having the spray bottle handy whenever or wherever jumping usually happens.

Yet a third method to discourage jumping is grasping the puppy's paws and holding them gently but firmly until he struggles to get away. Wait a brief moment or two, then release his paws and give him a command to sit. He should eventually learn that jumping gets him into an uncomfortable predicament.

Children are major victims of puppy jumping, since puppies view little people as ready targets for jumping up as well as nipping. If your children (or their friends) are unable to dispense jump corrections, you will have to intervene and handle it for them.

Important to prevention is also knowing what you should not do. Never kick your Chinese Crested (for any reason, not just for jumping) or knock him in the

**KEEP OUT OF REACH**

Most dogs don't browse around your medicine cabinet, but accidents do happen! The drug acetaminophen, the active ingredient in Tylenol®, can be deadly to dogs and cats if ingested in large quantities. Acetaminophen toxicity, caused by the dog's swallowing 15 to 20 tablets, can be manifested in abdominal pains within a day or two of ingestion, as well as liver damage. If you suspect your dog has swiped a bottle of Tylenol®, get the dog to the vet immediately so that the vet can induce vomiting and cleanse the dog's stomach.

chest with your knee. That maneuver could actually harm your puppy. Vets can tell you stories about puppies who suffered broken bones after being banged about when they jumped up.

### Puppy Whining

Puppies often cry and whine, just as infants and little children do. It's their way of telling us that they are lonely or in need of attention. Your puppy will miss his littermates and will feel insecure when he is left alone.

You may be out of the house or just in another room, but he will still feel alone. During these times, the puppy's crate should be his personal comfort station, a place all his own where he can feel safe and secure. Once he learns that being alone is okay and not something to be feared, he will settle down without crying or objecting. You might want to leave a radio on while he is crated, as the sound of human voices can be soothing and will give the impression that people are around.

Give your puppy a favorite

*The best time to lavish affection on your puppy is immediately after he has responded properly to a command.*

cuddly toy or chew toy to entertain him whenever he is crated. You will both be happier: the puppy because he is safe in his den and you because he is quiet, safe and not getting into puppy escapades that can wreak havoc in your house or cause him danger.

To make sure that your puppy will always view his crate as a safe and cozy place, never, ever, use the crate as punishment. That's the best way to turn the crate into a negative place that the pup will want to avoid. Sure, you can use the crate for your own peace of mind if your puppy is getting into trouble and needs some "time out." Just don't let him know that! Never scold the pup and immediately place him into the crate. Count to ten, give him a couple of hugs and maybe a treat, then scoot him into his crate.

It's also important not to make a big fuss when he is released from the crate. That will make getting out of the crate more appealing than being in the crate, which is just the opposite of what you are trying to achieve.

### FOOD GUARDING

Some dogs are picky eaters; others seem to inhale their food without chewing it. Occasionally the true "chow hound" will become protective of his food, which is one dangerous step toward other aggressive behavior. Food guarding is obvious: your puppy will growl, snarl or even attempt to bite you if you approach his food bowl or put your hand into his pan while he's eating.

This behavior is not acceptable, and very preventable! If your puppy is an especially voracious eater, sit next to him occasionally while he eats and dangle your fingers in his food bowl. Don't feed him in a corner, where he could feel possessive of his eating space. Rather, place his food bowl in an open area of your kitchen where you are in close proximity.

**THE FAMILY FELINE**

A resident cat has feline squatter's rights. The cat will treat the newcomer (your puppy) as she sees fit, regardless of what you do or say. So it's best to let the two of them work things out on their own terms. Cats have a height advantage and will generally leap to higher ground to avoid direct contact with a rambunctious pup. Some will hiss and boldly swat at a pup who passes by or tries to reach the cat. Keep the puppy under control in the presence of the cat and they will eventually become accustomed to each other.

Here's a hint: move the cat's litter box where the puppy can't get into it! It's best to do so well before the pup comes home so the cat is used to the new location.

Occasionally remove his food in mid-meal, tell him he's a good boy and return his bowl.

If your pup becomes possessive of his food, look for other signs of future aggression, like guarding his favorite toys or refusing to obey obedience commands that he knows. Consult an obedience trainer for help in reinforcing obedience so your Chinese Crested will fully understand that *you* are the boss.

A 12-week-old pup, all settled in his new home.

# CHINESE CRESTED

## FEEDING CONSIDERATIONS

A Chinese Crested should be fed sensibly on a high-quality diet, but an owner should never be tempted to allow the dog to put on too much weight. An overweight Chinese Crested can not only look rather unsightly but also can suffer health problems as a result, as indeed can any overweight dog. Most owners like to feed two small meals each day, but however frequently you decide to feed your dog, remember that no dog should ever be fed within an hour of strenuous exercise.

There are now numerous high-quality canine foods available, and one of them is sure to suit your Chinese Crested. If you have

*Once you have found a quality dry food that your Crested enjoys, you're well advised to stick to it for the duration of your dog's life.*

### THE BEST DIET

Feeding your dog the best diet is based on various factors, including age, activity level, overall condition and size of breed. When you visit the breeder, he will share with you his advice about the proper diet for your dog based on his experience with the breed and the foods with which he has had success. Likewise, your vet will be a helpful source of advice throughout the dog's life and will aid you in planning a diet for optimal health.

chosen your breeder well, you should be able to obtain sound advice from that breeder as to which food they consider most suitable. When you buy your puppy, the breeder should provide you with a diet sheet giving details of exactly how your puppy has been fed. Of course, you will be at liberty to change that food as the youngster reaches adulthood, but this should be done gradually.

It is important that small dogs, if fed on proprietary foods, are given "small bite" foods, for they will not be able to cope well with larger pieces. Some breeders also like to soak the food before feeding, especially if teeth are missing or loose.

Every breeder will have his own preference with regard to selection of food, but after the age of six months many select a lower protein diet than that which was given during the early months of life. Chicken-and-rice or lamb-and-rice diets seem to suit especially well. Chinese Cresteds that are susceptible to skin problems may find that if dairy products in the diet are kept to a bare minimum, it will help to alleviate the condition.

When selecting your dog's diet, three stages of development must be considered: the puppy stage, the adult stage and the senior or veteran stage.

### FEEDING THE PUPPY

Of course, your pup's very first food will be his dam's milk. There may be special situations in which pups fail to nurse, necessitating that the breeder hand-feed them with a formula, but for the most part pups spend the first weeks of life nursing from their dam. The breeder weans the pups by gradually introducing solid foods and decreasing the milk meals. Pups may even start themselves off on the weaning process, albeit inadvertently, if they snatch bites from their

### DIET DON'TS

- Got milk? Don't give it to your dog! Dogs cannot tolerate large quantities of cows' milk, as they do not have the enzymes to digest lactose.
- You may have heard of dog owners who add raw eggs to their dogs' food for a shiny coat or to make the food more palatable, but consumption of raw eggs too often can cause a deficiency of the vitamin biotin.
- Avoid feeding table scraps, as they will upset the balance of the dog's complete food. Additionally, fatty or highly seasoned foods can cause upset canine stomachs.
- Do not offer raw meat to your dog. Raw meat can contain parasites; it also is high in fat.
- Vitamin A toxicity in dogs can be caused by too much raw liver, especially if the dog already gets enough vitamin A in his balanced diet, which should be the case.
- Bones like chicken, pork chop and other soft bones are not suitable, as they easily splinter.

*Pups are given milk meals as part of the weaning process.*

mom's food bowl.

By the time the pups are ready for new homes, they are fully weaned and eating a good puppy food. As a new owner, you may be thinking, "Great! The breeder has taken care of the hard part." Not so fast.

A puppy's first year of life is the time when all or most of his growth and development takes place. This is a delicate time, and diet plays a huge role in proper skeletal and muscular formation. Improper diet and exercise habits can lead to damaging problems that will compromise the dog's health and movement for his entire life. That being said, new owners should not worry needlessly. With the myriad types of food formulated specifically for growing pups of different-sized breeds, dog-food manufacturers have taken much of the guesswork

out of feeding your puppy well. Since growth-food formulas are designed to provide the nutrition that a growing puppy needs, it is unnecessary and, in fact, can prove harmful to add supplements to the diet. Research has shown that too much of certain vitamin supplements and minerals predispose a dog to skeletal problems. It's by no means a case of "if a little is good, a lot is better." At every stage of your dog's life, too much or too little in the way of nutrients can be harmful, which is why a manufactured complete food is the easiest way to know that your dog is getting what he needs.

### VARIETY IS THE SPICE

Although dog-food manufacturers contend that dogs don't like variety in their diets, studies show quite the opposite to be true. Dogs would much rather vary their meals than eat the same old chow day in and day out. Dry kibble is no more exciting for a dog than the same bowl of bran flakes would be for you. Fortunately, there are dozens of varieties available on the market, and your dog will likely show preference for certain flavors over others. A word of warning: don't overdo it or you'll develop a fussy eater who only prefers chopped beef fillet and asparagus tips every night.

Puppies should be allowed to nurse from their mothers for the first six weeks and should be fully weaned by eight weeks of age.

Because of a young pup's small body and accordingly small digestive system, his daily portion will be divided up into small meals throughout the day. This can mean starting off with three or more meals a day and decreasing the number of meals as the pup matures. Eventually you can feed only one meal a day, although it is generally thought that dividing the day's food into two meals on a morning/evening schedule is healthier for the dog's digestion.

Regarding the feeding schedule, feeding the pup at the same times and in the same place each day is important for both housebreaking purposes and establishing the dog's everyday routine. As for the amount to feed, growing puppies generally need proportionately more food per body weight than their adult counterparts, but a pup should never be allowed to gain excess weight. Dogs of all ages should be kept in proper body condition, but extra weight can strain a pup's developing frame, causing skeletal problems.

Watch your pup's weight as he grows and, if the recommended amounts seem to be too much or too little for your pup, consult the vet about appropriate dietary changes. Keep in mind that treats, although small, can quickly add up throughout the day, contributing unnecessary calories. Treats are fine when used prudently; opt for dog treats specially formulated to be healthy or for nutritious snacks like small pieces of cheese or cooked chicken.

**FEEDING THE ADULT DOG**

For the adult (meaning physically mature) dog, feeding properly is about maintenance, not growth. Again, correct weight is a concern. Your dog should appear fit and should have an evident "waist." His ribs should not be protruding (a sign of being underweight), but they should be covered by only a slight layer of fat. Under normal circumstances, an adult dog can be maintained fairly easily with a high-quality nutritionally complete adult-formula food.

Factor treats into your dog's overall daily caloric intake, and avoid offering table scraps. Overweight dogs are more prone to health problems. Research has even shown that obesity takes years off a dog's life. With that in mind, resist the urge to overfeed and over-treat. Don't make unnecessary additions to your dog's diet, whether with tidbits or with extra vitamins and minerals.

The amount of food needed for proper maintenance will vary depending on the individual dog's activity level, but you will be able to tell whether the daily portions are keeping him in good shape. With the wide variety of good complete foods available, choosing what to feed is largely a matter of personal preference. Just as with the puppy, the adult dog should have consistency in his mealtimes and feeding place. In addition to a consistent routine, regular mealtimes also allow the owner to see how much his dog is eating. If the dog seems never to be satisfied or, likewise, becomes uninterested in his food, the owner will know right away that something is wrong and can consult the vet.

**DIETS FOR THE AGING DOG**

A good rule of thumb is that once a dog has reached 75% of his

---

**SWITCHING FOODS**

There are certain times in a dog's life when it becomes necessary to switch his food; for example, from puppy to adult food and then from adult to senior-dog food. Additionally, you may decide to feed your pup a different type of food from what he received from the breeder, and there may be "emergency" situations in which you can't find your dog's normal brand and have to offer something else temporarily. Anytime a change is made, for whatever reason, the switch must be done gradually. You don't want to upset the dog's stomach or end up with a picky eater who refuses to eat something new. A tried-and-true approach is, over the course of about a week, to mix a little of the new food in with the old, increasing the proportion of new to old as the days progress. At the end of the week, you'll be feeding his regular portions of the new food, and he will barely notice the change.

expected lifespan, he has reached "senior citizen" or geriatric status. Your Chinese Crested will be considered a senior at about 10 years of age; based on his size, he has a projected lifespan of about 13 years. (The smallest breeds generally enjoy the longest lives and the largest breeds the shortest.)

What does aging have to do with your dog's diet? No, he won't get a discount at the local diner's early-bird special. Yes, he will require some dietary changes to accommodate the changes that come along with increased age. One change is that the older dog's dietary needs become more similar to that of a puppy. Specifically, dogs can metabolize more protein as youngsters and seniors than in the adult-maintenance stage. Discuss with your vet whether you need to switch to a higher-protein or senior-formulated food or whether your current adult-dog food contains sufficient nutrition for the senior.

Watching the dog's weight remains essential, even more so in the senior stage. Older dogs are already more vulnerable to illness, and obesity only contributes to their susceptibility to problems. As the older dog becomes less active and, thus, exercises less, his regular portions may cause him to gain weight. At this point, you may consider decreasing his daily food intake or switching to a

**FREE FEEDING**

Many owners opt to feed their dogs the free way. That is, they serve dry kibble in a feeder that is available to the dog all day. Arguably, this is the most convenient method of feeding an adult dog, but it may encourage the dog to become fussy about food or defensive over his bowl. Free feeding is an option only for adult dogs, not puppies.

reduced-calorie food. As with other changes, you should consult your vet for advice.

TYPES OF FOOD AND READING THE LABEL

When selecting the type of food to feed your dog, it is important to check out the label for ingredients. Many dry-food products have soybean, corn or rice as the main ingredient. The main ingredient will be listed first on the label, with the rest of the ingredients following in descending order according to their proportion in the food. While these types of dry food are fine, you should also look into dry foods based on meat or fish. These are better-quality foods and thus higher priced. However, they may be just as economical in the long run, because studies have shown that it takes less of the higher-quality foods to maintain a dog.

Comparing the various types

of food, dry, canned and semi-moist, dry foods contain the least amount of water and canned foods the most. Proportionately, dry foods are the most calorie- and nutrient-dense, which means that you need more of a canned food product to supply the same amount of nutrition. In households domiciling breeds of disparate size, the canned/dry/semi-moist question can be of special importance. Larger breeds obviously eat more than smaller ones and thus in general do better on dry foods, but smaller breeds

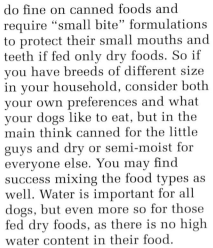

do fine on canned foods and require "small bite" formulations to protect their small mouths and teeth if fed only dry foods. So if you have breeds of different size in your household, consider both your own preferences and what your dogs like to eat, but in the main think canned for the little guys and dry or semi-moist for everyone else. You may find success mixing the food types as well. Water is important for all dogs, but even more so for those fed dry foods, as there is no high water content in their food.

There are strict controls that regulate the nutritional content of dog food, and a food has to meet the minimum requirements in order to be considered "complete and balanced." It is important that you choose such a food for your dog, so check the label to be sure that your chosen food meets the requirements. If not, look for a food that clearly states on the label that it is formulated to be complete and balanced for your dog's particular stage of life.

Recommendations for amounts to feed will also be indicated on the label. You should also ask your vet about proper food portions, and you will keep an eye on your dog's condition to see whether the recommended amounts are adequate. If he becomes over- or underweight, you will need to make adjustments; this also would be a good

## QUENCHING HIS THIRST

Is your dog drinking more than normal and trying to lap up everything in sight? Excessive drinking has many different causes. Obvious causes for a dog's being thirstier than usual are hot weather and vigorous exercise. However, if your dog is drinking more for no apparent reason, you could have cause for concern. Serious conditions like kidney or liver disease, diabetes and various types of hormonal problems can all be indicated by excessive drinking. If you notice your dog's being excessively thirsty, contact your vet at once. Hopefully there will be a simpler explanation, but the earlier a serious problem is detected, the sooner it can be treated, with a better rate of cure.

time to consult your vet.

The food label may also make feeding suggestions, such as whether moistening a dry-food product is recommended. Sometimes a splash of water will make the food more palatable for the dog and even enhance the flavor. Don't be overwhelmed by the many factors that go into feeding your dog. Manufacturers of complete and balanced foods make it easy, and once you find the right food and amounts for your Chinese Crested, his daily feeding will be a matter of routine.

### DON'T FORGET THE WATER!

For a dog, it's always time for a drink! Regardless of what type of food he eats, there's no doubt that he needs plenty of water. Fresh cold water, in a clean bowl, should be freely available to your dog at all times. There are special circumstances, such as during puppy housebreaking, when you will want to monitor your pup's water intake so that you will be able to predict when he will need to relieve himself, but water must be available to him nonetheless. Water is essential for hydration and proper body function just as it is in humans.

You will get to know how much your dog typically drinks in a day. Of course, in the heat or if exercising vigorously, he will be more thirsty and will drink more.

However, if he begins to drink noticeably more water for no apparent reason, this could signal any of various problems, and you are advised to consult your vet.

Water is the best drink for dogs. Some owners are tempted to give milk from time to time or to moisten dry food with milk, but dogs do not have the enzymes necessary to digest the lactose in milk, which is much different from the milk that nursing puppies receive. Therefore stick with clean fresh water to quench your dog's thirst, and always have it readily available to him.

### EXERCISE

Chinese Cresteds, although small, are active; they require and thoroughly enjoy exercise. They will usually be more than happy to be taken for on-lead walks, and will also enjoy a free run, though owners should be careful that the areas in which their dogs exercise

*Puppies, adult and senior Chinese Cresteds all have benefited from the wide range of nutritious and appealing foods available to dogs today.*

are thoroughly safe. Keep in mind that a Chinese Crested is likely to stand its ground against other dogs, and a meeting with a large aggressive dog may not be a happy one!

Keep in mind, too, that Chinese Cresteds in general are very proficient jumpers. In consequence, when given freedom off the lead, in the yard or even around the home, they are capable of jumping higher walls and fences than might be expected.

Not all Chinese Crested owners live in houses with gardens, but those that do often find that their dogs exercise themselves quite happily on their own grounds, especially if more than one dog is kept in the family. For those owners living in apartments, regular on-lead walks are necessary.

To keep any breed of dog healthy, it is essential that opportunity be given to build up muscle tone. This important part of canine care should never be overlooked, even in a breed as small as the Chinese Crested. Likewise, bear in mind that an overweight dog should never be suddenly over-exercised; instead he should be encouraged to increase exercise slowly. Not only is exercise essential to keep the dog's body fit, it is essential to his mental well-being. A bored dog will find something to do, which often manifests itself in some type

of destructive behavior. In this sense, exercise is essential for the owner's mental well-being as well!

## GROOMING

### SKIN AND COAT MAINTENANCE
There is rather more in the way of coat maintenance for a Powderpuff than for a Hairless Chinese Crested, but both will need to be bathed fairly frequently to keep skin and coat in good condition. It must be stressed that although it is always important to rinse thoroughly after shampooing, this is especially so in the case of the Hairless variety.

Some owners of Hairless dogs like to rub them down with glycerine immediately following a bath to prevent the skin from becoming too dry. It is also wise to apply a suitable cream on the body quite frequently to maintain the skin's suppleness. The skin

---

**DOGGIE SPF**

Modern science has emphasized the importance of sunscreen for ourselves and taking precautions in the sun. Some of these principles apply to dogs, too. Chinese Crested Hairless require sunblock lotion whenever they are outdoors. Powderpuffs usually only require protection on exposed areas such as the nose, ears and belly. A sunblock lotion should be at least SPF 35 for the Chinese Crested.

quality on Chinese Cresteds varies, so each owner will undoubtedly find the type of moisturizing agent that best suits his or her own dog.

Some Hairless Chinese Cresteds grow hair in places where it is not desirable. If this is the case, unwanted areas of hair growth are often carefully and discreetly removed. The method of removal is very much a matter of personal preference, but some owners like to use a mustache/ beard trimmer, which is both inexpensive and relatively quiet.

In a Powderpuff, any mats or tangles in the coat must always be carefully removed prior to bathing. Although the Powderpuff is long coated, this is by no means a difficult coat to maintain; a thorough weekly brush and comb will usually be sufficient for good condition.

The plumes of hair on head, ears, feet and tail of a Hairless should be carefully groomed through regularly. This will keep any mats from forming and enable the plumage to hang freely.

### BATHING

In general, dogs need to be bathed only a few times a year, but the Chinese Crested requires bathing at least once a month. Show dogs are usually bathed before every show, which could be as frequent as weekly, although this depends on the owner. Bathing too

Even as an adult, the Chinese Crested is conveniently sized for bathing in a sink.

frequently can have negative effects on the skin and coat, removing natural oils and causing dryness.

If you give your dog his first bath when he is young, he will become accustomed to the process. Wrestling a dog into the tub or chasing a freshly shampooed dog who has escaped from the bath will be no fun! Most dogs don't naturally enjoy their baths, but you at least want yours to cooperate with you.

Before bathing the dog, have the items you'll need close at hand. First, decide where you will bathe the dog. You should have a tub or basin with a non-slip surface. Your Chinese Crested can be bathed in a sink. In warm

The plumes (head, feet, tail) on the Hairless should be brushed through regularly to prevent mats and to encourage the fringe to fall freely.

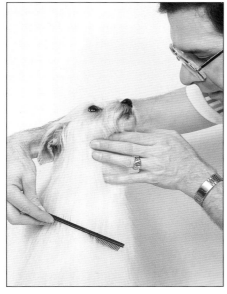

The Powderpuff's coat, though long, is easy to maintain with regular brushing and combing.

weather, some like to use a portable pool in the yard, although you'll want to make sure your dog doesn't head for the nearest dirt pile following his bath! You will also need a hose or shower spray to wet the Powderpuff's coat thoroughly, a shampoo formulated for dogs, absorbent towels and perhaps a blow dryer. Human shampoos are too harsh for dogs' coats and will dry them out.

Before wetting the Powderpuff, give him a brush-through to remove any dead hair, dirt and mats. Make sure he is at ease in the tub and have the water at a comfortable temperature. Begin bathing by wetting the coat all the way down to the skin. Massage in the shampoo, keeping it away from his face and eyes. Rinse him thoroughly, again avoiding the eyes and ears, as you don't want to get water into the ear canals. A thorough rinsing is important, as shampoo residue is drying and itchy to the dog. After rinsing, wrap him in a towel to absorb the initial moisture. You can finish drying with either a towel or a blow dryer on low heat, held at a safe distance from the dog. You should keep the dog indoors and away from drafts until he is completely dry.

### EAR CLEANING
While keeping your dog's ears clean unfortunately will not cause

him to "hear" your commands any better, it will protect him from ear infection and ear-mite infestation. In addition, a dog's ears are vulnerable to waxy build-up and to collecting foreign matter from the outdoors. Look in your dog's ears regularly to ensure that they look pink, clean and otherwise healthy. Even if they look fine, an odor in the ears signals a problem and means it's time to call the vet.

A dog's ears should be cleaned regularly; once a week is suggested, and you can do this along with your regular brushing. Using a cotton ball or pad, and never probing into the ear canal, wipe the ear gently. You can use an ear-cleansing liquid or powder available from your vet or pet-supply store; alternatively, you might prefer to use home-made solutions with ingredients like one part white vinegar and one part hydrogen peroxide. Ask your vet about home remedies before you attempt to concoct something on your own!

Keep your Chinese Crested's ears free of excess hair by plucking it as needed. If done gently, this will be painless for the dog. Look for wax, brown droppings (a sign of ear mites), redness or any other abnormalities. At the first sign of a problem, contact your vet so that he can prescribe an appropriate medication.

Cream is applied to the Hairless's skin, both after bathing to prevent dryness and before an appearance in the show ring to give the skin a smooth, supple look.

Cleaning these ears is serious business! It is not advisable to probe into the ear with a cotton bud, as shown here, but rather to use a soft wipe and ear cleaner made for dogs.

The key to
getting the
cooperation of
your Chinese
Crested in the
nail-maintenance
process is to start
him out in it as a
puppy.

### TOENAIL MAINTENANCE

Care should always be taken that toenails are in good condition and not causing any discomfort, but the Chinese Crested's nails are usually kept somewhat longer than those of other breeds, in accordance with the breed standard. Before trimming your Crested's nails, consult a breeder or groomer to learn the correct moderate length at which you should maintain them.

Having his nails trimmed is not on many dogs' lists of favorite things to do. With this in mind, you will need to accustom your puppy to the procedure at a young age so that he will sit still (well, as still as he can) for his pedicures. Long nails can cause the dog's feet to spread, which is not good for him; likewise, long nails can hurt if they unintentionally scratch, not good for you!

Some dogs' nails are worn down naturally by regular walking on hard surfaces, so the frequency with which you clip depends on your individual dog. Look at his nails from time to time and clip as needed; a good way to know when it's time for a trim is if you hear your dog clicking as he walks across the floor.

There are several types of nail clippers and even electric nail-grinding tools made for dogs; first we'll discuss using the clipper. To start, have your clipper ready and some doggie treats on hand. You want your pup to view his nail-clipping sessions in a positive light, and what better way to convince him than with food? You may want to enlist the help of an assistant to comfort the pup and offer treats as you concentrate on the clipping itself. The guillotine-type clipper is thought of by many as the easiest type to use; the nail tip is inserted into the opening, and blades on the top and bottom snip it off in one clip.

Start by grasping the pup's paw; a little pressure on the foot pad causes the nail to extend, making it easier to clip. Clip off a little at a time. If you can see the "quick," which is a blood vessel that runs through each nail, you will know how much to trim, as you do not want to cut into the quick. On that note, if you do cut the quick, which will cause bleeding, you can stem the flow of blood with a styptic pencil or other clotting agent. If you mistakenly nip the quick, do not panic or fuss, as this will cause the pup to be afraid. Simply reassure the pup, stop the bleeding and move on to the next nail. Don't be discouraged; you will become a professional canine pedicurist with practice.

You may or may not be able to see the quick, so it's best to just clip off a small bit at a time. If you see a dark dot in the center of the nail, this is the quick and your cue to stop clipping. Tell the puppy he's a "good boy" and offer a piece of treat with each nail. You can also use nail-clipping time to examine the footpads, making sure that they are not dry and cracked and that nothing has become embedded in them.

The nail grinder, the second choice, is many owners' first choice. Accustoming the puppy to the sound of the grinder and sensation of the buzz presents fewer challenges than the clipper, and there's no chance of cutting through the quick. Use the grinder on a low setting and always talk soothingly to your dog. He won't mind his salon visit, and he'll have nicely polished nails as well.

## A Clean Smile

Since dentition problems and missing teeth are commonly seen in Cresteds, it's essential for owners to take a proactive role in their dogs' dental health. Studies show that around 80% of dogs experience dental problems by two years of age, and the percentage is higher in older dogs. Therefore it is highly likely that your dog will have trouble with his teeth and gums unless you are proactive with home dental care.

The most common dental problem in dogs is plaque build-up. If not treated, this causes gum disease, infection and resultant tooth loss. Bacteria from these infections spread throughout the body, affecting the vital organs. Do you need much more convincing to start brushing your dog's teeth? If so, take a good whiff of your dog's breath, and read on.

Fortunately, home dental care is rather easy and convenient for pet owners. Specially formulated

**As you can see, scraping the teeth can necessitate a three-handed approach—and not every owner wants to get involved with the process.**

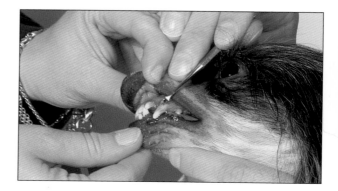

canine toothpaste is easy to find. You should use one of these toothpastes, not a product for humans. Some doggie pastes are even available in flavors appealing to dogs. If your dog likes the flavor, he will tolerate the process better, making things much easier for you! Doggie toothbrushes come in different sizes and are designed to fit the contour of a canine mouth. Rubber fingertip brushes fit right on one of your fingers and have rubber nodes to clean the teeth and massage the gums. This may be easier to handle, as it is akin to rubbing your dog's teeth with your finger.

## IDENTIFICATION AND TRAVEL

### ID FOR YOUR DOG

You love your Chinese Crested and want to keep him safe. Of course you take every precaution to prevent his escaping from the yard or becoming lost or stolen. You have a sturdy high fence and you always keep your dog on lead when out and about in public

Take care of your Hairless's delicate skin in the sun; some owners like to use a cream that contains sunscreen.

## BEAT THE HEAT

Summertime means outdoor activity for the whole family, including your favorite canine companion. Before you throw your dog headlong into a routine of summer activity, some caution is advised to avoid heat-related health problems. Dogs can be affected by heat exhaustion and/or heat stroke caused by stress from high temperatures and poor ventilation. Although the Chinese Crested sweats, unlike coated breeds, it still can overheat on a hot day. Heat stroke is the more serious of the two and can be fatal. Heat exhaustion usually occurs after long periods of vigorous exercise in intense heat. Symptoms include panting, rapid heartbeat, staring expression and vomiting. The dog may collapse. Also touch his body; does his skin feel warm and dry? Take his temperature if possible. The Crested's body temperature is higher than that of other dogs, being 104° F; a dog's normal temperature range is between 100.5 and 102.5° F; affected dogs' temperatures can be 105° F and higher.

If symptoms appear, the dog needs to be cooled down immediately, followed by a trip to the vet. Immersion in cold water, either in a tub or with a hose if no tub is available, is the best way to do this; ice packs around the head and neck may also help. Once his temperature is lowered, get to the vet's clinic.

places. If your dog is not properly identified, however, you are overlooking a major aspect of his safety. We hope to never be in a situation where our dog is missing, but we should practice prevention in the unfortunate case that this happens; identification greatly increases the chances of your dog's being returned to you

There are several ways to identify your dog. First, the traditional dog tag should be a staple in your dog's wardrobe, attached to his everyday collar. Tags can be made of sturdy plastic and various metals and should include your contact information so that a person who finds the dog can get in touch with you right away to arrange his return. Many people today enjoy the wide range of decorative tags available, so have fun and create a tag to match your dog's personality. Of course, it is important that the tag stays on the collar, so have a secure "O" ring attachment; you also can explore the type of tag that slides right onto the collar.

In addition to the ID tag, which every dog should wear even if identified by another method, two other forms of identification have become popular: microchipping and tattooing. In microchipping, a tiny scannable chip is painlessly inserted under the dog's skin. The number is registered to you so that, if your lost dog turns up at a clinic or shelter, the chip can be scanned to retrieve your contact information.

The advantage of the microchip is that it is a permanent form of ID, but there are some factors to consider. Several different companies make microchips, and not all are compatible with the others' scanning devices. It's best to find a company with a universal microchip that can be read by scanners made by other companies as well. It won't do any good to have the dog chipped if the information cannot be retrieved. Also, not every humane society, shelter and clinic is equipped with a scanner, although more and more facilities are equipping themselves. In fact,

## CAN I COME, TOO?

Your dog can accompany you most anywhere you go. A picnic in the park and the kids' Little League game are just two examples of outdoor events where dogs likely will be welcome. Of course, your dog will need to be kept on lead or safely crated in a well-ventilated crate. Bring along your "doggie bag" with all of the supplies you will need, like water, food or treats and a stash of plastic bags or other clean-up aids. Including your dog in the family activities is fun for all of you, providing excellent owner/dog quality time and new socialization opportunities.

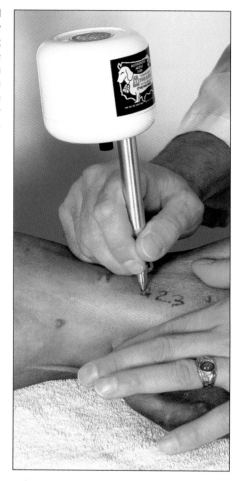

Chinese Crested being tattooed by the vet. Tattooing is a more permanent form of identification than the more common collar and ID tag.

many shelters microchip dogs that they adopt out to new homes.

In the US, there are five or six major microchip manufacturers as well as a few databases. The American Kennel Club's Companion Animal Recovery unit works in conjunction with HomeAgain™ Companion Animal Retrieval System (Schering-Plough). In the UK, The Kennel Club is affiliated with the National Pet Register, operated by Wood Green Animal Shelters.

Because the microchip is not visible to the eye, the dog must wear a tag that states that he is microchipped so that whoever picks him up will know to have him scanned. He of course also should have a tag with contact information in case his chip cannot be read. Humane societies and veterinary clinics offer this service, which is usually very affordable.

Though less popular than microchipping, tattooing is another permanent method of ID for dogs. Most vets perform this service, and there are also clinics that perform dog tattooing. This is also an affordable procedure and one that will not cause much discomfort for the dog. It is best to put the tattoo in a visible area, such as the ear, to deter theft. It is sad to say that there are cases of dogs' being stolen and sold to research laboratories, but such laboratories will not accept tattooed dogs.

To ensure that the tattoo is effective in aiding your dog's return to you, the tattoo number must be registered with a national organization. That way, when someone finds a tattooed dog a phone call to the registry will quickly match the dog with his owner.

## HIT THE ROAD

Car travel with your Chinese Crested may be limited to necessity only, such as trips to the vet, or you may bring your dog along almost everywhere you go. This will depend much on your individual dog and how he reacts to rides in the car. You can begin desensitizing your dog to car travel as a pup so that it's something that he's used to. Still, some dogs suffer from motion sickness. Your vet may prescribe a medication for this if trips in the car pose a problem for your dog. At the very least, you will need to get him to the vet, so he will need to tolerate these trips with the least amount of hassle possible.

Start taking your pup on short trips, maybe just around the block to start. If he is fine with short trips, lengthen your rides a little at a time. Start to take him on your errands or just for drives around town. By this time it will be easy to tell whether your dog is a born traveler or would prefer staying at home when you are on the road.

Of course, safety is a concern for dogs in the car. First, he must travel securely, not left loose to roam about the car where he could be injured or distract the driver. A young pup can be held by a passenger initially but should soon graduate to a travel crate, which can be the same crate he uses in the home. Other options

A suitable dog tag will assist someone who finds a lost dog in reuniting the dog with his owners.

include a car harness (like a seat belt for dogs) and partitioning the back of the car with a gate made for this purpose.

Bring along what you will need for the dog. He should wear his collar and ID tags, of course, and you should bring his leash, water (and food if a long trip) and clean-up materials for potty breaks and in case of motion sickness. Always keep your dog on his leash when you make stops, and never leave him alone in the car. Many a dog has died from the heat inside a closed car; this does not take much time at all. A dog left alone inside a car can also be a target for thieves.

# TRAINING YOUR

# CHINESE CRESTED

## BASIC TRAINING PRINCIPLES: PUPPY VS. ADULT

There's a big difference between training an adult dog and training a young puppy. With a young puppy, everything is new. At 10 to 12 weeks of age, he will be experiencing many things, and he has nothing with which to compare these experiences. Up to this point, he has been with his dam and littermates, not one-on-one with people except in his interactions with his breeder and visitors to the litter.

When you first bring the puppy home, he is eager to please you. This means that he accepts doing things your way. During the next couple of months, he will absorb the basis of everything he needs to know for the rest of his life. This early age is even referred to as the "sponge" stage. After

A well-trained Chinese Crested embodies grace, intelligence and good behavior, and will be a wonderful companion with whom to share your home.

that, for the next 18 months, it's up to you to reinforce good manners by building on the foundation that you've established. Once your puppy is reliable in basic commands and behavior and has reached the appropriate age, you may gradually introduce him to some of the interesting sports, games and activities available to pet owners and their dogs.

Raising your puppy is a family affair. Each member of the family must know what rules to set forth for the puppy and how to use the same one-word commands to mean exactly the same thing every time. Even if yours is a large family, one person will soon be considered by the pup to be the leader, the Alpha person in his pack, the "boss" who must be obeyed. Often that highly regarded person turns out to be the one who feeds the puppy. Food ranks very high on the puppy's list of important things! That's why your puppy is rewarded with small treats along with verbal praise when he responds to you correctly. As the puppy learns to do what you want him to do, the food rewards are gradually eliminated and only the praise remains. If you were to keep up with the food treats, you could have two problems on your hands—an obese dog and a beggar.

Training begins the minute

## THE RIGHT START

The best advice for a potential dog owner is to start with the very best puppy that money can buy. Don't shop around for a bargain in the newspaper. You're buying a companion, not a used Buick or a second-hand Maytag. The purchase price of the dog represents a very significant part of the investment, but this is indeed a very small sum compared to the expenses of maintaining the dog in good health. If you purchase a well-bred healthy and sound puppy, you will be starting right. An unhealthy puppy can cost you thousands of dollars in unnecessary veterinary expenses and, possibly, a fortune in heartbreak as well.

**OUR CANINE KIDS**

"Everything I learned about parenting, I learned from my dog." How often adults recognize that their parenting skills are mere extensions of the education they acquired while caring for their dogs. Many owners refer to their dogs as their "kids" and treat their canine companions like real members of the family. Surveys indicate that a majority of dog owners talk to their dogs regularly, celebrate their dogs' birthdays and purchase Christmas gifts for their dogs. Another survey shows that dog owners take their dogs to the veterinarian more frequently than they visit their own physicians.

and telling him by your actions to "Go for it! Run wild!" Even if this is your first puppy, you must act as if you know what you're doing: be the boss. An uncertain pup may be terrified to move, while a bold one will be ready to take you at your word and start plotting to destroy the house! Before you collected your puppy, you decided where his own special place would be, and that's where to put him when you first arrive home. Give him a house tour after he has investigated his area and had a nap and a bathroom "pit stop."

It's worth mentioning here that, if you've adopted an adult dog that is completely trained to your liking, lucky you! You're off the hook! However, if that dog spent his life up to this point in a kennel, or even in a good home but without any real training, be prepared to tackle the job ahead. A dog three years of age or older with no previous training cannot be blamed for not knowing what he was never taught. While the dog is trying to understand and learn your rules, at the same time he has to unlearn many of his previously self-taught habits and general view of the world.

Working with a professional trainer will speed up your progress with an adopted adult dog. You'll need patience, too. Some new rules may be close to impossible for the dog to accept. After all, he's been successful so

your Chinese Crested puppy steps through the doorway of your home, so don't make the mistake of putting the puppy on the floor far by doing everything his way! (Patience again.) He may agree with your instruction for a few days and then slip back into his old ways, so you must be just as consistent and understanding in your teaching as you would be with a puppy. (More patience needed yet again!) Your dog has to learn to pay attention to your voice, your family, the daily routine, new smells, new sounds and, in some cases, even a new climate.

One of the most important things to find out about a newly adopted adult dog is his reaction to children (yours and others), strangers and your friends, and how he acts upon meeting other dogs. If he was not socialized with dogs as a puppy, this could be a major problem. This does not mean that he's a "bad" dog, a vicious dog or an aggressive dog; rather, it means that he has no idea how to read another dog's body language. There's no way for him to tell whether the other dog is a friend or foe. Survival instinct takes over, telling him to attack first and ask questions later. This definitely calls for professional help and, even then, may not be a behavior that can be corrected 100% reliably (or even at all). If you have a puppy, this is why it is so very important to introduce your young puppy properly to other puppies and "dog-friendly" adult dogs.

## HOUSE-TRAINING YOUR CHINESE CRESTED

When it comes to house-training, dogs respond to the surface on which they are given approval to eliminate. The choice is yours (the dog's version is in parentheses): The lawn (including the neighbors' lawns)? A bare patch of earth under a tree (where people like to sit and relax in the summertime)? Concrete steps or patio (all sidewalks, garage and basement floors)? The curbside

Whether you are housebreaking an adult or a puppy, you must monitor the dog's water intake closely. Never offer a full bowl of water at bedtime.

remember? Starting out by paper-training often is the only choice for a city dog.

**WHEN YOUR PUPPY'S "GOT TO GO"**
Your puppy's need to relieve himself is seemingly non-stop, but signs of improvement will be seen each week. From 8 to 10 weeks old, the puppy will have to be taken outside every time he wakes up, about 10-15 minutes after every meal and after every period

*Don't overdo treats when training your Crested. A well-deserved tidbit won't go unappreciated.*

(watch out for cars)? A small area of crushed stone in a corner of the yard (mine!)? The latter is the best choice if you can manage it, because it will remain strictly for the dog's use and is easy to keep clean.

You can start out with paper-training indoors and switch over to an outdoor surface as the puppy matures and gains control over his need to eliminate. For the nay-sayers, don't worry—this won't mean that the dog will soil on every piece of newspaper lying around the house. You are training him to go outside,

*Once your puppy is older he should be used to the routine of being led outside for his potty trips.*

**HOUSE-TRAINING SIGNALS**
Watch your puppy for signs that he has to relieve himself (sniffing, circling and squatting), and waste no time in whisking him outside to do his business. Once the puppy is older, you should attach his leash and head for the door. Puppies will always "go" immediately after they wake up, within minutes after eating and after brief periods of play, but young puppies should also be taken out regularly at times other than these, just in case! If necessary, set a timer to remind you to take him out.

of play—all day long, from first thing in the morning until his bedtime! That's a total of ten or more trips per day to teach the puppy where it's okay to relieve himself. With that schedule in mind, you can see that house-training a young puppy is not a part-time job. It requires someone to be home all day.

If that seems overwhelming or impossible, do a little planning. For example, plan to pick up your puppy at the start of a vacation period. If you can't get home in the middle of the day, plan to hire a dog-sitter or ask a neighbor to come over to take the pup outside, feed him his lunch and then take him out again about ten or so minutes after he's eaten. Also make arrangements with that or another person to be your "emergency" contact if you have to stay late on the job. Remind yourself—repeatedly—that this hectic schedule improves as the puppy gets older.

### HOME WITHIN A HOME

Your Chinese Crested puppy needs to be confined to one secure, puppy-proof area when no one is able to watch his every move. Generally the kitchen is the place of choice because the floor is washable. Likewise, it's a busy family area that will accustom the pup to a variety of noises, everything from pots and pans to the telephone, blender and dishwasher. He will also be enchanted by the smell of your cooking (and will never be critical when you burn something). An exercise pen (also called an "ex-pen," a puppy version of a playpen) within the room of choice is an excellent means of

### CONFINEMENT

It is wise to keep your puppy confined to a small "puppy-proofed" area of the house for his first few weeks at home. Gate or block off a space near the door he will use for outdoor potty trips. Expandable baby gates are useful to create puppy's designated area. If he is allowed to roam through the entire house or even only several rooms, it will be more difficult to house-train him.

confinement for a young pup. He can see out and has a certain amount of space in which to run about, but he is safe from dangerous things like electrical cords, heating units, trash baskets or open kitchen-supply cabinets. Place the pen where the puppy will not get a blast of heat or air conditioning.

In the pen, you can put a few toys, his bed (which can be his crate if the dimensions of pen and crate are compatible) and a few

Condominium and apartment dwellers often have no choice about whether to paper-train their puppies.

layers of newspaper in one small corner, just in case. A water bowl can be hung at a convenient height on the side of the ex-pen so it won't become a splashing pool for an innovative puppy. His food dish can go on the floor, near but not under the water bowl.

> ### EXTRA! EXTRA!
> The headlines read: "Puppy Piddles Here!" Breeders commonly use newspapers to line their whelping pens, so puppies learn to associate newspapers with relieving themselves. Do not use newspapers to line your pup's crate, as this will signal to your puppy that it is OK to urinate in his crate. If you choose to paper-train your puppy, you will layer newspapers on a section of the floor near the door he uses to go outside. You should encourage the puppy to use the papers to relieve himself, and bring him there whenever you see him getting ready to go. Little by little, you will reduce the size of the newspaper-covered area so that the puppy will learn to relieve himself "on the other side of the door."

Crates are something that pet owners are at last getting used to for their dogs. Wild or domestic canines have always preferred to sleep in den-like safe spots, and that is exactly what the crate provides. How often have you seen adult dogs that choose to sleep under a table or chair even though they have full run of the house? It's the den connection.

In your "happy" voice, use the word "Crate" every time you put the pup into his den. If he's new to a crate, toss in a small biscuit for him to chase the first few times. At night, after he's been outside, he should sleep in his crate. The crate may be kept in his designated area at night or, if you want to be sure to hear those wake-up yips in the morning, put the crate in a corner of your bedroom. However, don't make any response whatsoever to whining or crying. If he's completely ignored, he'll settle down and get to sleep.

Good bedding for a young puppy is an old folded bath towel or an old blanket, something that is easily washable and disposable if necessary ("accidents" will happen!). Never put newspaper in the puppy's crate. Also those old ideas about adding a clock to replace his mother's heartbeat, or

a hot-water bottle to replace her warmth, are just that—old ideas. The clock could drive the puppy nuts, and the hot-water bottle could end up as a very soggy waterbed! An extremely good breeder would have introduced your puppy to the crate by letting two pups sleep together for a couple of nights, followed by several nights alone. How thankful you will be if you found that breeder!

Safe toys in the pup's crate or area will keep him occupied, but monitor their condition closely. Discard any toys that show signs of being chewed to bits. Squeaky parts, bits of stuffing or plastic or any other small pieces can cause intestinal blockage or possibly choking if swallowed.

**PROGRESSING WITH POTTY-TRAINING**
After you've taken your puppy out and he has relieved himself in the area you've selected, he can have some free time with the family as long as there is someone responsible for watching him. That doesn't mean just someone in the same room who is watching TV or busy on the computer, but one person who is doing nothing other than keeping an eye on the pup, playing with him on the floor and helping him understand his position in the pack.

This first taste of freedom will let you begin to set the house rules. If you don't want the dog

### ESTABLISH A ROUTINE
Routine is very important to a puppy's learning environment. To facilitate house-training, use the same exit/entrance door for potty trips and always take the puppy to the same place in the yard. The same principle of consistency applies to all other aspects of puppy training.

on the furniture, now is the time to prevent his first attempts to jump up onto the couch. The word to use in this case is "Off," not "Down." "Down" is the word you will use to teach the down position, which is something entirely different.

Most corrections at this stage come in the form of simply distracting the puppy. Instead of telling him "No" for "Don't chew the carpet," distract the chomping puppy with a toy and he'll forget about the carpet.

As you are playing with the pup, do not forget to watch him closely and pay attention to his body language. Whenever you see him begin to circle or sniff, take the puppy outside to relieve himself. If you are paper-training, put him back into his confined area on the newspapers. In either case, praise him as he eliminates while he actually is in the act of relieving himself. Three seconds after he has finished is too late! You'll be praising him for running toward you, or picking up a toy or whatever he may be doing at that moment, and that's not what you want to be praising him for. Timing is a vital tool in all dog training. Use it.

Remove soiled newspapers immediately and replace them with clean ones. You may want to take a small piece of soiled paper and place it in the middle of the new clean papers, as the scent will attract him to that spot when it's time to go again. That scent attraction is why it's so important to clean up any messes made in the house by using a product

> ### TIDY BOY
> Clean by nature, dogs do not like to soil their dens, which in effect are their crates or sleeping quarters. Unless not feeling well, dogs will not defecate or urinate in their crates. Crate training capitalizes on the dog's natural desire to keep his den clean. Be conscientious about giving the puppy as many opportunities to relieve himself outdoors as possible. Reward the puppy for correct behavior. Praise him and pat him whenever he "goes" in the correct location. Even the tidiest of puppies can have potty accidents, so be patient and dedicate more energy to helping your puppy achieve a clean lifestyle.

specially made to eliminate the odor of dog urine and droppings. Regular household cleansers won't do the trick. Pet shops sell the best pet deodorizers. Invest in the largest container you can find.

Scent attraction eventually will lead your pup to his chosen spot outdoors; this is the basis of outdoor training. When you take your puppy outside to relieve himself, use a one-word command such as "Outside" or "Go-potty" (that's one word to the puppy!) as you pick him up and attach his leash. Then put him down in his area. If for any reason you can't carry him, snap the leash on

**Your Chinese Crested's keen sense of smell plays a large part in his being successfully house-trained.**

quickly and lead him to his spot. Now comes the hard part—hard for you, that is. Just stand there until he urinates and defecates. Move him a few feet in one direction or another if he's just sitting there looking at you, but remember that this is neither playtime nor time for a walk. This is strictly a business trip! Then, as he circles and squats (remember your timing!), give him a quiet "Good dog" as praise. If you start to jump for joy, ecstatic over his performance, he'll do one of two things: either he will stop midstream, as it were, or he'll do it again for you—in the house—and expect you to be just as delighted!

Give him five minutes or so and, if he doesn't go in that time, take him back indoors to his confined area and try again in another ten minutes, or immediately if you see him sniffing and circling. By careful observation,

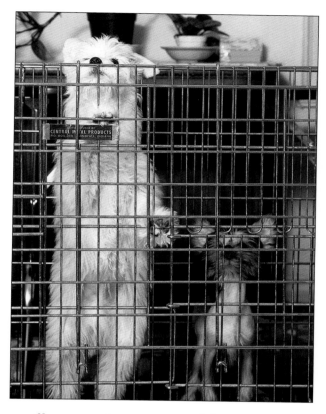

## LITTER BOXES

If necessary, Chinese Cresteds can be trained to use a litter box, but you should not expect your cat to share her bathroom. For owners who are away from the house for more than four hours at a time, this is a real option. Cresteds can quickly learn to use the litter, almost as quickly as a cat learns. If you are unable to crate-train your dog, the litter box provides a nice alternative to paper-training.

you'll soon work out a successful schedule.

Accidents, by the way, are just that—accidents. Clean them up quickly and thoroughly, without comment, after the puppy has been taken outside to finish his business and then put back into his area or crate. If you witness an accident in progress, say "No!" in a stern voice and get the pup outdoors immediately. No punishment is needed. You and your puppy are just learning each other's language, and sometimes

Setting limits is a necessary element of training. Gates used as partitions can help to define your dog's designated areas within the home.

it's easy to miss a puppy's message. Chalk it up to experience and watch more closely from now on.

**KEEPING THE PACK ORDERLY**
Discipline is a form of training that brings order to life. For example, military discipline is what allows the soldiers in an army to work as one. Discipline is a form of teaching and, in dogs, is the basis of how the successful pack operates. Each member knows his place in the pack and all respect the leader, or Alpha dog. It is essential for your puppy that you establish this type of relationship, with you as the Alpha, or leader. It is a form of social coexistence that all canines recognize and accept. Discipline, therefore, is never to be confused with punishment. When you teach your puppy how you want him to behave, and he behaves properly and you praise him for it, you are disciplining him with a form of positive reinforcement.

For a dog, rewards come in the form of praise, a smile, a cheerful tone of voice, a few friendly pats or a rub of the ears. Rewards are also small food treats. Obviously, that does not mean bits of regular dog food. Instead, treats are very small bits of special things like cheese or pieces of soft dog treats. The idea is to reward the dog with something very small that he can taste and swallow, providing instant positive reinforcement. If he has to take time to chew the treat, by the time he is finished he will have forgotten what he did to earn it!

Your puppy should never be physically punished. The displeasure shown on your face and in your voice is sufficient to signal to the pup that he has done something wrong. He wants to please everyone higher up on the social ladder, especially his leader, so a scowl and harsh voice will take care of the error. Growling out the word "Shame!" when the pup is caught in the act of doing something wrong is better than the repetitive "No." Some dogs hear "No" so often that they begin to think it's their name!

**SMILE WHEN YOU ORDER ME AROUND!**
While trainers recommend practicing with your dog every day, it's perfectly acceptable to take a "mental health day" off. It's better not to train the dog on days when you're in a sour mood. Your bad attitude or lack of interest will be sensed by your dog, and he will respond accordingly. Studies show that dogs are well tuned in to their humans' emotions. Be conscious of how you use your voice when talking to your dog. Raising your voice or shouting will only erode your dog's trust in you as his trainer and master.

### KEEP IT SIMPLE—AND FUN

Practicing obedience is not a military drill. Keep your lessons simple, interesting and user-friendly. Fun breaks help you both. Spend two minutes or ten teaching your puppy, but practice only as long as your dog enjoys what he's doing and is focused on pleasing you. If he's bored or distracted, stop the training session after any correct response (always end on a high note!). After a few minutes of playtime, you can go back to "hitting the books."

By the way, do not use the dog's name when you're correcting him. His name is reserved to get his attention for something pleasant about to take place.

There are punishments that have nothing to do with you. For example, your dog may think that chasing cats is one reason for his existence. You can try to stop it as much as you like but without success, because it's such fun for the dog. But one good hissing, spitting, swipe of a cat's claws across the dog's nose will put an end to the game forever. Intervene only when your dog's eyeball is seriously at risk. Cat scratches can cause permanent damage to an innocent but annoying puppy.

## PUPPY KINDERGARTEN

### COLLAR AND LEASH

Before you begin your Chinese Crested puppy's education, he must be used to his collar and leash. Choose a collar for your puppy that is secure, but not heavy or bulky. He won't enjoy training if he's uncomfortable. A flat buckle collar is fine for everyday wear and for initial puppy training. For older dogs, there are several types of training collars such as the martingale, which is a double loop that tightens slightly around the neck, or the head collar, which is

Nothing gets a pup's attention more quickly than a tasty tidbit! But make sure you offer praise and gradually phase out the treats in your training routine.

similar to a horse's halter. Do not use a chain choke collar unless you have been specifically shown how to put it on and how to use it. You may not be disposed to use a chain choke collar even if your breeder has told you that it's suitable for your Chinese Crested.

A lightweight 6-foot woven cotton or nylon training leash is preferred by most trainers because it is easy to fold up in your hand and comfortable to hold because there is a certain amount of give to it. There are lessons where the dog will start off 6 feet away from you at the end of the leash. The leash used to take the puppy outside to relieve himself is shorter because you don't want him to roam away from his area. The shorter leash will also be the one to use when you walk the puppy.

If you've been fortunate enough to enroll in a Puppy Kindergarten training class, suggestions will be made as to the best collar and leash for your young puppy. I say "fortunate" because your puppy will be in a class with puppies in his age range (up to five months old) of all breeds and sizes. It's the perfect way for him to learn the right way (and the wrong way) to interact with other dogs as well as their people. You cannot teach your puppy how to interpret another dog's sign language. For a first-time puppy owner, these socialization classes are invaluable. For experienced dog owners, they are a real boon to further training.

### ATTENTION

You've been using the dog's name since the minute you collected him from the breeder, so you should be able to get his attention by saying his name—with a big smile and in an excited tone of voice. His response will be the puppy equivalent of "Here I am! What are we going to do?" Your immediate response (if you haven't guessed by now) is "Good dog." Rewarding him at the moment he pays attention to you teaches him the proper way to respond when he hears his name.

## EXERCISES FOR A BASIC CANINE EDUCATION

### THE SIT EXERCISE

There are several ways to teach the puppy to sit. The first one is to catch him whenever he is about to sit and, as his backside nears the floor, say "Sit, good dog!" That's positive reinforcement and, if your timing is sharp, he will learn that what he's doing at that second is connected to your saying "Sit" and that you think he's clever for doing it!

Another method is to start with the puppy on his leash in front of you. Show him a treat in the palm of your right hand. Bring your hand up under his nose and, almost in slow motion, move your hand up and back so his nose goes up in the air and his head tilts back as he follows the treat in your hand. At that point, he will have to either sit or fall over, so as his back legs buckle under, say "Sit, good dog," and then give him the treat and lots of praise. You may have to begin with your hand lightly running up his chest, actually lifting his chin up until he sits. Some (usually older) dogs require gentle pressure on their hindquarters with the left hand, in which case the dog should be on your left side. Puppies generally do not appreciate this physical dominance.

After a few times, you should be able to show the dog a treat in the open palm of your hand, raise your hand waist-high as you say "Sit" and have him sit. Once

"Sit" is a very good place to start. Practice this lesson indoors and out until your Crested is completely reliable.

again, you have taught him two things at the same time. Both the verbal command and the motion of the hand are signals for the sit. Your puppy is watching you almost more than he is listening to you, so what you do is just as important as what you say.

Don't save any of these drills only for training sessions. Use them as much as possible at odd times during a normal day. The dog should always sit before being given his food dish. He should sit to let you go through a doorway first, when the doorbell rings or when you stop to speak to someone on the street.

### SIT AROUND THE HOUSE

"Sit" is the command you'll use most often. Your pup objects when placed in a sit with your hands, so try the "bringing the food up under his chin" method. Better still, catch him in the act! Your dog will sit on his own many times throughout the day, so let him know that he's doing the "Sit" by rewarding him. Praise him and have him sit for everything—toys, connecting his leash, his dinner, before going out the door, etc.

### THE DOWN EXERCISE

Before beginning to teach the down command, you must

consider how the dog feels about this exercise. To him, "down" is a submissive position. Being flat on the floor with you standing over him is not his idea of fun. It's up to you to let him know that, while it may not be fun, the reward of your approval is worth his effort.

Start with the puppy on your left side in a sit position. Hold the leash right above his collar in your left hand. Have an extra-special treat, such as a small piece of cooked chicken or hot dog, in your right hand. Place it at the end of the pup's nose and steadily move your hand down and forward along the ground. Hold the leash to prevent a sudden lunge for the food. As the puppy

*The down position is not one that your Chinese Crested will relish initially, but he can be coaxed into it once you have earned his trust.*

**DON'T STRESS ME OUT**

Your dog doesn't have to deal with paying the bills, the daily commute, PTA meetings and the like, but, believe it or not, there's a lot of stress in a dog's world. Stress can be caused by the owner's impatient demeanor and his angry or harsh corrections. If your dog cringes when you reach for his training collar, he's stressed. An older dog is sometimes stressed out when he goes to a new home. No matter what the cause, put off all training until he's over it. If he's going through a fear period—shying away from people, trembling when spoken to, avoiding eye contact or hiding under furniture—wait to resume training. Naturally you'd also postpone your lessons if the dog were sick, and the same goes for you. Show some compassion.

goes into the down position, say "Down" very gently.

The difficulty with this exercise is twofold: it's both the submissive aspect and the fact that most people say the word "Down" as if they were a drill sergeant in charge of recruits! So issue the command sweetly, give him the treat and have the pup maintain the down position for several seconds. If he tries to get up immediately, place your hands on his shoulders and press down gently, giving him a very quiet "Good dog." As you progress with this lesson, increase the "down time" until he will hold it until you say "Okay" (his cue for release). Practice this one in the house at various times throughout the day.

By increasing the length of time during which the dog must maintain the down position, you'll find many uses for it. For example, he can lie at your feet in the vet's office or anywhere that both of you have to wait, when you are on the phone, while the family is eating and so forth. If you progress to training for competitive obedience, he'll already be all set for the exercise called the "long down."

### THE STAY EXERCISE

You can teach your Chinese Crested to stay in the sit, down and stand positions. To teach the sit/stay, have the dog sit on your left side. Hold the leash at waist level in your left hand and let the dog know that you have a treat in your closed right hand. Step forward on your right foot as you say "Stay." Immediately turn and stand directly in front of the dog, keeping your right hand up high so he'll keep his eye on the treat hand and maintain the sit position for a count of five. Return to your original position and offer the reward.

Increase the length of the sit/stay each time until the dog can hold it for at least 30 seconds

without moving. After about a week of success, move out on your right foot and take two steps before turning to face the dog. Give the "Stay" hand signal (left palm back toward the dog's head)

### TEACHER'S PET

Dogs are individuals, not robots, with many traits basic to their breed. Some, bred to work alone, are independent thinkers; others rely on you to call the shots. If you have enrolled in a training class, your instructor can offer alternative methods of training based on your individual dog's instincts and personality. You may benefit from using a different type of collar or switching to a class with different kinds of dogs.

as you leave. He gets the treat when you return and he holds the sit/stay. Increase the distance that you walk away from him before turning until you reach the length of your training leash. But don't rush it! Go back to the beginning if he moves before he should. No matter what the lesson, never be upset by having to back up for a few days. The repetition and practice are what will make your dog reliable in these commands. It won't do any good to move on to something more difficult if the command is not mastered at the easier levels. Above all, even if you do get frustrated, never let your puppy know! Always keep a positive, upbeat attitude during training, which will transmit to

## HOW DO I GET TO CARNEGIE HALL?

Or the National Obedience Championships? The same way you get your dog to do anything else—practice, practice, practice. It's *how* you practice that counts. Keep sessions short, varied, interesting and interspersed with active fun. A bored dog isn't learning. If you're feeling out of sorts yourself, quit for the day. Set yourself a reasonable schedule for several brief practice sessions every day and stick to it. Practice randomly throughout the day as you're doing different things around the house. Lots of praise for that good "Sit" in front of the TV or while waiting for his dinner!

Cresteds live for their owners' praise and approval. A loving pat and a kind word lead you and your dog toward a trusting relationship.

your dog for positive results.

The down/stay is taught in the same way once the dog is completely reliable and steady with the down command. Again, don't rush it. With the dog in the down position on your left side, step out on your right foot as you say "Stay." Return by walking around in back of the dog and into your original position. While you are training, it's okay to murmur something like "Hold on" to encourage him to stay put. When the dog will stay without moving when you are at a distance of 3 or 4 feet, begin to increase the length of time before you return. Be sure he holds the down on your return until you say "Okay." At that point, he gets his treat–just so he'll remember for next time that it's not over until it's over.

Make your Chinese Crested feel completely relaxed in the down/stay position. Reward him after he's stayed for two or three minutes.

### THE COME EXERCISE

No command is more important to the safety of your Chinese Crested than "come." It is what you should say every single time you see the puppy running toward you: "Binky, come! Good dog." During playtime, run a few feet away from the puppy and turn and tell him to "come" as he is already running to you. You can go so far as to teach your puppy two things at once if you squat down and hold out your arms. As the pup gets close to you and you're saying "Good dog," bring your right arm in about waist high. Now he's also learning the hand signal, an excellent device should you be on the phone when you need to get him to come to you! You'll also both be one step

## I WILL FOLLOW YOU

Obedience isn't just a classroom activity. In your home you have many great opportunities to teach your dog polite manners. Allowing your pet on the bed or furniture elevates him to your level, which is not a good idea (the word is "Off!"). Use the "umbilical cord" method, keeping your dog on lead so he has to go with you wherever you go. You sit, he sits. You walk, he heels. You stop, he sit-stays. Everywhere you go, he's with you, but you go first!

## MORE PRAISE, LESS FOOD

As you progress with your puppy's lessons, and the puppy is responding well, gradually begin to wean him off the treats by alternating the treats with times when you offer only verbal praise or a few pats on the dog's side. (Pats on the head are dominant actions, so he won't think they are meant to be praise.) Every lesson should end with the puppy's performing the correct action for that session's command. When he gets it right and you withhold the treat, the praise can be as long and lavish as you like. The commands are one word only, but your verbal praise can use as many words as you want...don't skimp!

ahead when you enter obedience classes.

Puppies, like children, have notoriously short attention spans, so don't overdo it with any of the training. Keep each lesson short. Break it up with a quick run around the yard or a ball toss, repeat the lesson and quit as soon as the pup gets it right. That way, you will always end with a "Good dog."

When the puppy responds to your well-timed "Come," try it with the puppy on the training leash. This time, catch him off guard, while he's sniffing a leaf or watching a bird: "Binky, come!" You may have to pause for a split second after his name to be sure you have his attention. If the puppy shows any sign of confusion, give the leash a mild jerk and take a couple of steps backward. Do not repeat the command. In this case, you should say "Good come" as he reaches you.

That's the number-one rule of training. Each command word is given just once. Anything more is nagging. You'll also notice that all commands are one word only. Even when they are actually two words, you say them as one.

Never call the dog to come to you—with or without his name—if you are angry or intend to correct him for some misbehavior. When correcting the pup, you go to him. Your dog must always connect "come" with something pleasant and with your approval; then you can rely on his response.

Life isn't perfect and neither are puppies. A time will come, often around 10 months of age, when he'll become "selectively deaf" or choose to "forget" his name. He may respond by wagging his tail (and even seeming to smile at you) with a look that says "Make me!" Laugh, throw his favorite toy and skip the lesson you had planned. Pups will be pups!

### THE HEEL EXERCISE

The second most important command to teach, after the come, is the heel. When you are walking your growing puppy, you need to be in control. Besides, it looks terrible to be pulled and yanked down the street, and it's not much fun either. Your ten-week-old

The great outdoors may present too many enticing smells, sounds and other sensations to be a viable place to practice heel training with your Crested.

puppy will probably follow you everywhere, but that's his natural instinct, not your control over the situation. However, any time he does follow you, you can say "Heel" and be ahead of the game, as he will learn to associate this command with the action of following you before you even begin teaching him to heel.

There is a very precise, almost military, procedure for teaching your dog to heel. As with all other obedience training, begin with the dog on your left side. He will be in a very nice sit and you will have the training leash across your chest. Hold the loop and folded leash in your right hand. Pick up the slack leash above the

---

### LET'S GO!

Many people use "Let's go" instead of "Heel" when teaching their dogs to behave on lead. It sounds more like fun! When beginning to teach the heel, whatever command you use, always step off on your left foot. That's the one next to the dog, who is on your left side, in case you've forgotten. Keep a loose leash. When the dog pulls ahead, stop, bring him back and begin again. Use treats to guide him around turns.

dog in your left hand and hold it loosely at your side. Step out on your left foot as you say "Heel." If the puppy does not move, give a gentle tug or pat your left leg to get him started. If he surges ahead of you, stop and pull him back

### TIME TO PLAY!

Playtime can happen both indoors and out. A young puppy is growing so rapidly that he needs sleep more than he needs a lot of physical exercise. Puppies get sufficient exercise on their own just through normal puppy activity. Monitor play with young children so you can remove the puppy when he's had enough, or calm the kids if they get too rowdy. Almost all puppies love to chase after a toy you've thrown, and you can turn your games into educational activities. Every time your puppy brings the toy back to you, say "Give it" (or "Drop it") followed by "Good dog" and throwing it again. If he's reluctant to give it to you, offer a small treat so that he drops the toy as he takes the treat. He will soon get the idea.

gently until he is at your side. Tell him to sit and begin again.

Walk a few steps and stop while the puppy is correctly beside you. Tell him to sit and give mild verbal praise. (More enthusiastic praise will encourage him to think the lesson is over.) Repeat the lesson, increasing the number of steps you take only as long as the dog is heeling nicely beside you. When you end the lesson, have him hold the sit, then give him the "Okay" to let him know that this is the end of the lesson. Praise him so that he knows he did a good job.

The cure for excessive pulling (a common problem) is to stop when the dog is no more than 2 or 3 feet ahead of you. Guide him back into position and begin again. With a really determined puller, try switching to a head collar. This will automatically turn the pup's head toward you so

you can bring him back easily to the heel position. Give quiet, reassuring praise every time the leash goes slack and he's staying with you.

Staying and heeling can take a lot out of a dog, so provide playtime and free-running exercise to shake off the stress when the lessons are over. You don't want him to associate training with all work and no fun.

**TAPERING OFF TIDBITS**

Your dog has been watching you—and the hand that treats— throughout all of his lessons, and now it's time to break the treat habit. Begin by giving him treats at the end of each lesson only. Then start to give a treat after the end of only some of the lessons. At the end of every lesson, as well as during the lessons, be consis-

tent with the praise. Your pup now doesn't know whether he'll get a treat or not, but he should keep performing well just in case! Finally, you will stop giving treat rewards entirely. Save them for something brand-new that you want to teach him. Keep up the praise and you'll always have a "good dog."

**Do not attempt to train your dog in areas that hold many distractions.**

**OBEDIENCE CLASSES**

The advantages of an obedience class are that your dog will have to learn amid the distractions of other people and dogs and that your mistakes will be quickly

**KIDS RULE**

Children of 10 to 12 year of age are old enough to understand the "be kind to dumb animals" approach and will have fun training their dogs, especially to do tricks. It teaches them to be tolerant, patient and appreciative as well as to accept failure to some extent. Young children can be tyrants, making unreasonable demands on the dog and unable to cope with defeat, blaming it all on the dog. Toddlers need not apply.

Here's top
breeder Arleen
Butterklee
showing one of
her flawless
Powderpuffs. A
reputation for
excellence in the
breed ring only
comes from hard
work, talent and
dedication.

corrected by the trainer. Teaching your dog along with a qualified instructor and other handlers who may have more dog experience than you is another plus of the class environment. The instructor and other handlers can help you to find the most efficient way of teaching your dog a command or exercise. It's often easier to learn by other people's mistakes than your own. You will also learn all of the requirements for competitive obedience trials, in which

Here's top breeder Arleen Butterklee showing one of her flawless Powderpuffs. A reputation for excellence in the breed ring only comes from hard work, talent and dedication.

A "well-heeled" Crested struts his stuff on the end of the lead in the show ring, where dogs often have to heel at their handlers' right side.

you can earn titles and go on to advanced jumping and retrieving exercises, which are fun for many dogs. Obedience classes build the foundation needed for many other canine activities (in which we humans are allowed to participate, too!).

## TRAINING FOR OTHER ACTIVITIES

Once your dog has basic obedience under his collar and is 12 months of age, you can enter the world of agility training. Dogs think agility is pure fun, like being turned loose in an amusement park full of obstacles! In addition to agility, there are hunting activities for sporting dogs, lure-coursing events for sighthounds, go-to-ground events for terriers, racing for the Nordic sled dogs, herding trials for the shepherd breeds and tracking, which is open to all "nosey" dogs (which would include all dogs!). For those who like to volunteer, there is the wonderful feeling of owning a therapy dog and visiting hospices, nursing homes and veterans' homes to bring smiles, comfort and companion-ship to those who live there.

Around the house, your Chinese Crested can be taught to do some simple chores. You might teach him to carry a basket of household items or to fetch the morning newspaper. The kids can teach the dog all kinds of tricks, from playing hide-and-seek to balancing a biscuit on his nose. A family dog is what rounds out the family. Everything he does beyond sitting in your lap or gazing lovingly at you represents the bonus of owning a dog.

A successful day in the ring for both dog and owner.

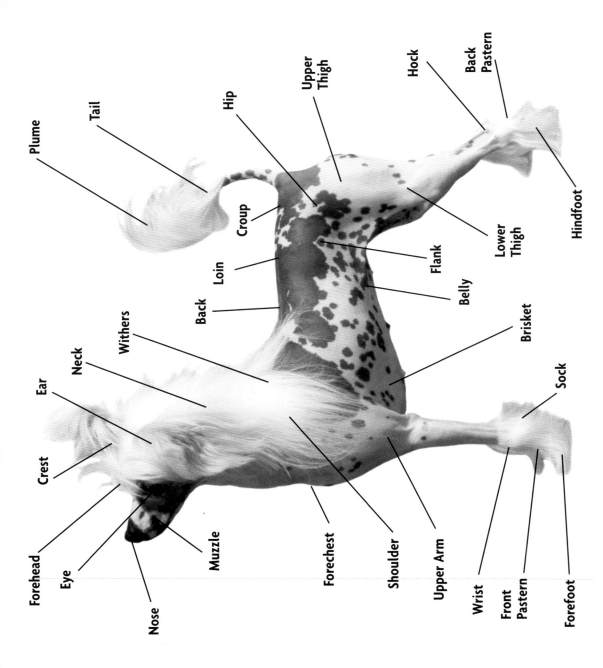

Plume

Tail

Hip

Upper Thigh

Hock

Back Pastern

Croup

Lower Thigh

Hindfoot

Loin

Flank

Back

Belly

Withers

Neck

Brisket

Ear

Crest

Sock

Forehead

Muzzle

Eye

Forechest

Shoulder

Upper Arm

Wrist

Front Pastern

Forefoot

Nose

# PHYSICAL STRUCTURE OF THE CHINESE CRESTED

# HEALTHCARE OF YOUR

# CHINESE CRESTED

## By Lowell Ackerman DVM, DACVD

**HEALTHCARE FOR A LIFETIME**

When you own a dog, you become his healthcare advocate over his entire lifespan, as well as being the one to shoulder the financial burden of such care. Accordingly, it is worthwhile to focus on prevention rather than treatment, as you and your pet will both be happier.

Of course, the best place to have begun your program of preventive healthcare is with the initial purchase or adoption of your dog. There is no way of guaranteeing that your new furry friend is free of medical problems, but there are some things you can do to improve your odds. You certainly should have done adequate research into the Chinese Crested and have selected your puppy carefully rather than buying on impulse. Health issues aside, a large number of pet abandonment and relinquishment cases arise from a mismatch between pet needs and owner expectations. This is entirely preventable with appropriate planning and finding a good breeder.

Regarding healthcare issues specifically, it is very difficult to make blanket statements about where to acquire a problem-free pet, but, again, a reputable breeder is your best bet. In an ideal situation you have the opportunity to see both parents, get references from other owners of the breeder's pups and see genetic-testing documentation for several generations of the litter's ancestors. At the very least, you must thoroughly investigate the Chinese Crested and the problems inherent in the breed, as well as the genetic testing available to screen for those problems. Genetic testing offers some important benefits, but testing is available for only a few disorders in a relatively small number of breeds and is not available for some of the most common genetic diseases, such as hip dysplasia, cataracts, epilepsy, cardiomyopathy, etc. This area of research is indeed exciting and increasingly important, and advances will continue to be made each year. In fact, recent research has shown that there is an equivalent dog gene for 75% of known human genes, so research done in either species is likely to benefit the other.

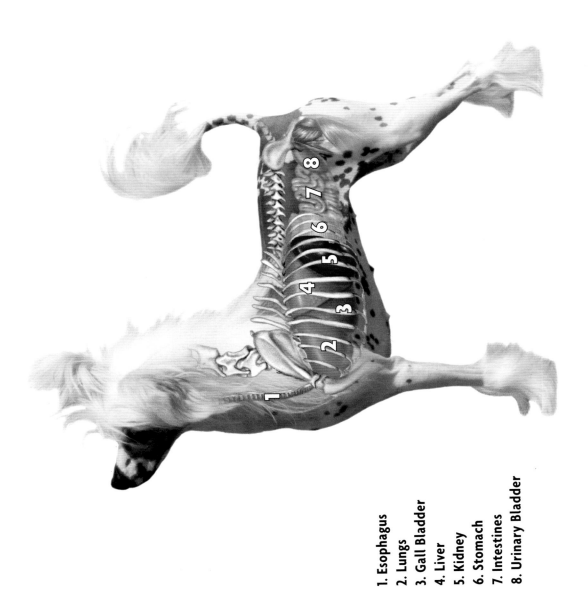

1. Esophagus
2. Lungs
3. Gall Bladder
4. Liver
5. Kidney
6. Stomach
7. Intestines
8. Urinary Bladder

# INTERNAL ORGANS OF THE CHINESE CRESTED

We've also discussed that evaluating the behavioral nature of your Chinese Crested and that of his immediate family members is an important part of the selection process that cannot be underestimated or overemphasized. It is sometimes difficult to evaluate temperament in puppies because certain behavioral tendencies, such as some forms of aggression, may not be immediately evident. More dogs are euthanized each year for behavioral reasons than for all medical conditions combined, so it is critical to take temperament issues seriously. Start with a well-balanced, friendly companion and put the time and effort into proper socialization, and you will both be rewarded with a lifelong valued relationship.

Assuming that you have started off with a pup from healthy, sound stock, you then become responsible for helping your veterinarian keep your pet healthy. Some crucial things happen before you even bring your puppy home. Parasite control typically begins at two weeks of age, and vaccinations typically begin at six to eight weeks of age. A pre-pubertal evaluation is typically scheduled for about six months of age. At this time, a dental evaluation is done (since the adult teeth are now in), heartworm prevention is started and neutering or spaying

## HOME DENTAL PLAN

It is critical to commence regular dental care at home if you have not already done so. It may not sound very important, but most dogs have active periodontal disease by four years of age if they don't have their teeth cleaned regularly at home, not just at their veterinary exams. Dental problems lead to more than just bad "doggie breath": gum disease can have very serious medical consequences. If you start brushing your dog's teeth and using antiseptic rinses from a young age, your dog will be accustomed to it and will not resist. The results will be healthy dentition, which your pet will need to enjoy a long, healthy life.

is most commonly done.

Most dogs are considered adults at a year of age, although some larger breeds still have some filling out to do up to about two or so years old. Even individual dogs within each breed have different healthcare requirements, so work with your veterinarian to determine what will be needed and what your role should be. This doctor-client relationship is important, because as vaccination guidelines change, there may not be an annual "vaccine visit" scheduled. You must make sure that you see your veterinarian at least annually, even if no vaccines are due, because this is the best

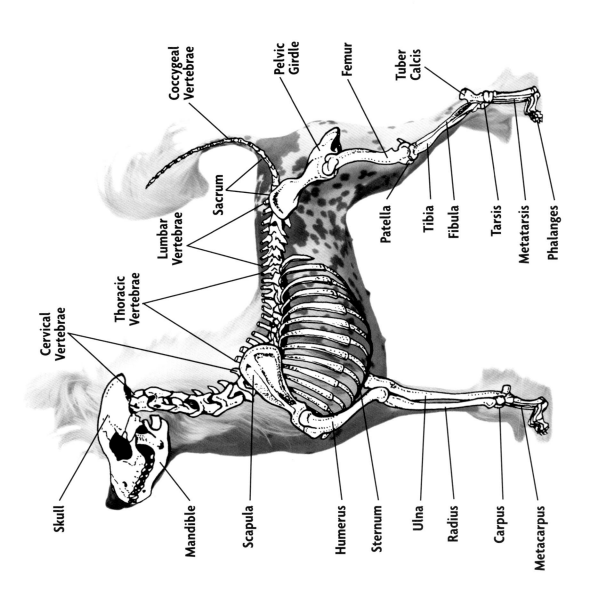

Coccygeal Vertebrae

Pelvic Girdle

Femur

Tuber Calcis

Sacrum

Lumbar Vertebrae

Patella

Tibia

Fibula

Tarsis

Metatarsis

Phalanges

Thoracic Vertebrae

Cervical Vertebrae

Skull

Mandible

Scapula

Humerus

Sternum

Ulna

Radius

Carpus

Metacarpus

# SKELETAL STRUCTURE OF THE CHINESE CRESTED

opportunity to coordinate healthcare activities and to make sure that no medical issues creep by unaddressed.

When your Chinese Crested reaches three-quarters of his anticipated lifespan, he is considered a "senior" and likely requires some special care. In general, if you've been taking great care of your canine companion throughout his formative and adult years, the transition to senior status should be a smooth one. Age is not a disease, and as long as everything is functioning as it should, there is no reason why most of late adulthood should not be rewarding for both you and your pet. This is especially true if you have tended to the details, such as regular veterinary visits, proper dental care, excellent nutrition and management of bone and joint issues.

At this stage in your Chinese Crested's life, your veterinarian may want to schedule visits twice yearly, instead of once, to run some laboratory screenings, electrocardiograms and the like, and to change the diet to something more digestible. Catching problems early is the best way to manage them effectively. Treating the early stages of heart disease is so much easier than trying to intervene when there is more significant damage to the heart muscle.

Similarly, managing the beginning of kidney problems is fairly routine if there is no significant kidney damage. Other problems, like cognitive dysfunction (similar to senility and Alzheimer's disease), cancer, diabetes and arthritis, are more common in older dogs, but all can be treated to help the dog live as many happy, comfortable years as possible. Just as in people, medical management is more effective (and less expensive) when you catch things early.

## SELECTING A VETERINARIAN

There is probably no more important decision that you will make regarding your pet's healthcare than the selection of his doctor. Your pet's veterinarian will be a pediatrician, family-practice physician and gerontologist,

### DOGGIE DENTAL DON'TS

A veterinary dental exam is necessary if you notice one or any combination of the following in your dog:
- Broken, loose or missing teeth
- Loss of appetite (which could be due to mouth pain or illness caused by infection)
- Gum abnormalities, including redness, swelling and bleeding
- Drooling, with or without blood
- Yellowing of the teeth or gumline, indicating tartar
- Bad breath

It is helpful if your vet can perform additional services such as tattooing.

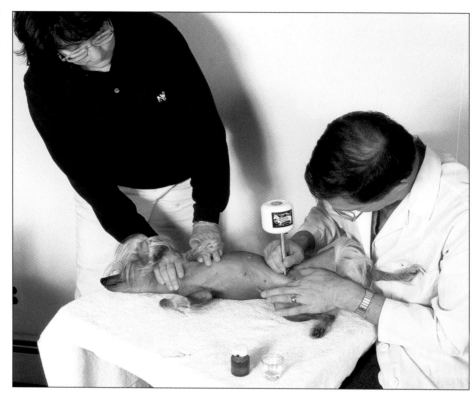

The vet is not just your dog's doctor, but his dentist as well. Your dog should have routine dental exams just as you do.

depending on the dog's life stage, and will be the individual who makes recommendations regarding issues such as when specialists need to be consulted, when diagnostic testing and/or therapeutic intervention is needed and when you will need to seek outside emergency and critical-care services. Your vet will act as your advocate and liaison throughout these processes.

Everyone has his own idea about what to look for in a vet, an individual who will play a big role in his dog's (and, of course, his own) life for many years to come. For some, it is the compassionate caregiver with whom they hope to develop a professional relationship to span the lifetime of their dogs and even their future pets. For others, they are seeking a clinician with keen diagnostic and therapeutic insight who can deliver state-of-the-art healthcare. Still others need a veterinary facility that is open evenings and weekends, or is in close proximity or provides mobile veterinary services, to accommodate their schedules; these people may not much mind that their dogs might see different veterinarians on each visit. Just as we have different reasons for selecting our own healthcare professionals (e.g., covered by insurance plan, expert in field, convenient location, etc.), we should not expect that there is a one-size-fits-all recommendation for selecting a veterinarian and veterinary practice. The best advice is to be honest in your assessment of what you expect from a veterinary practice and to conscientiously research the options in your area. You will quickly appreciate that not all veterinary practices are the same, and you will be happiest with one that truly meets your needs.

There is another point to be considered in the selection of veterinary services. Not that long ago, a single veterinarian would attempt to manage all medical and surgical issues as they arose. That was often problematic, because

## SPECIALISTS NOT SO SPECIAL

There are now many types of veterinary specialists, including dermatologists, cardiologists, ophthalmologists, surgeons, internists, oncologists, neurologists, behaviorists, criticalists and others to help primary-care veterinarians deal with complicated medical challenges. In most cases, specialists see cases referred by primary-care veterinarians, make diagnoses and set up management plans. From there, the animals' ongoing care is returned to their primary-care veterinarians. This important team approach to your pet's medical-care needs has provided opportunities for advanced care and an unparalleled level of quality to be delivered.

veterinarians are trained in many species and many diseases, and it was just impossible for general veterinary practitioners to be experts in every species, every field and every ailment. However, just as in the human healthcare fields, specialization has allowed general practitioners to concentrate on primary healthcare delivery, especially wellness and the prevention of infectious diseases, and to utilize a network of specialists to assist in the management of conditions that require specific expertise and experience.

**INSURE YOUR CRESTED**

Pet insurance policies are very cost-effective (and very inexpensive by human health-insurance standards), but make sure that you buy the policy long before you intend to use it (preferably starting in puppyhood, because coverage will exclude pre-existing conditions) and that you are actually buying an indemnity insurance plan from an insurance company that is regulated by your state or province. Many insurance policy look-alikes are actually discount clubs that are redeemable only at specific locations and for specific services. An indemnity plan covers your pet at almost all veterinary, specialty and emergency practices and is an excellent way to manage your pet's ongoing healthcare needs.

With all of the opportunities for your Chinese Crested to receive high-quality veterinary medical care, there is another topic that needs to be addressed at the same time—cost. It's been said that you can have excellent healthcare or inexpensive healthcare, but never both; this is as true in veterinary medicine as it is in human medicine. While veterinary costs are a fraction of what the same services cost in the human healthcare arena, it is still difficult to deal with unanticipated medical costs, especially since they can easily creep into hundreds or even thousands of dollars if specialists or emergency services become involved. However, there are ways of managing these risks. The easiest is to buy pet health insurance and realize that its foremost purpose is not to cover routine healthcare visits but rather to serve as an umbrella for those rainy days when your pet needs medical care and you don't want to worry about whether or not you can afford that care.

## VACCINATIONS AND INFECTIOUS DISEASES

There has never been an easier time to prevent a variety of infectious diseases in your dog, but the advances we've made in veterinary medicine come with a price—choice. Now while it may seem that choice is a good thing (and it is), it has never been more difficult for the pet owner (or the veterinarian) to make an informed decision about the best way to protect pets through vaccination.

Years ago, it was just accepted that puppies got a starter series of vaccinations and then annual "boosters" throughout their lives to keep them protected. As more and more vaccines became available, consumers wanted the convenience of having all of that protection in a single injection. The result was "multivalent" vaccines that crammed a lot of protection into a single syringe. The manufacturers' recommendations were to give the vaccines annually, and this was a simple enough protocol to follow. However, as veterinary medicine has become more sophisticated and we have started looking more at healthcare quandaries rather than convenience, it became necessary to reevaluate the situation and deal with some tough questions. It is important to realize that whether or not to use a particular vaccine depends on the risk of contracting the disease against which it protects, the severity of the disease if it is contracted, the duration of immunity provided by the vaccine, the safety of the product and the needs of the individual animal. In a very general sense, rabies, distemper, hepatitis and parvovirus are considered core

## ARE VACCINATIONS NECESSARY?

Vaccinations are recommended for all puppies by the American Veterinary Medical Association (AVMA). Some vaccines are absolutely necessary, while others depend upon a dog's or puppy's individual exposure to certain diseases or the animal's immune history. Rabies vaccinations are required by law in all 50 states. Some diseases are fatal whereas others are treatable, making the need for vaccinating against the latter questionable. Follow your veterinarian's recommendations to keep your dog fully immunized and protected. You can also review the AVMA directive on vaccinations on their website: www.avma.org.

vaccine needs, while parainfluenza, *Bordetella bronchiseptica*, leptospirosis, coronavirus and borreliosis (Lyme disease) are considered non-core needs and best reserved for animals that demonstrate reasonable risk of contracting the diseases.

**THE GREAT VACCINATION DEBATE**
What kinds of questions need to be addressed? When the vet injects multiple organisms at the same time, might some of the components interfere with one another in the development of

immunologic protection? We don't have the comprehensive answer for that question, but it does appear that the immune system better handles agents when given individually. Unfortunately, most manufacturers still bundle their vaccine components because that is what most pet owners want, so getting vaccines with single components can sometimes be difficult.

Another question has to do with how often vaccines should be given. Again, this seems to be different for each vaccine component. There seems to be a general consensus that a puppy (or a dog with an unknown vaccination history) should get a series of vaccinations to initially stimulate his immunity and then a booster at one year of age, but even the veterinary associations and colleges have trouble reaching agreement about what he should get after that. Rabies vaccination schedules are not debated, because vaccine schedules for this contagious and devastating disease are determined by government agencies. Regarding the rest, some recommend that we continue to give the vaccines annually because this method has worked well as a disease preventive for decades and delivers predictable protection. Others recommend that some of the vaccines need to be given only every second or third year, as this

can be done without affecting levels of protection. This is probably true for some vaccine components (such as hepatitis), but there have been no large studies to demonstrate what the optimal interval should be and whether the same principles hold true for all breeds.

It may be best to just measure titers, which are protective blood levels of various vaccine components, on an annual basis, but that too is not without controversy. Scientists have not precisely determined the minimum titer of specific vaccine components that will be guaranteed to provide a pet with protection. Pets with very high titers will clearly be protected and those with very low titers will need repeat vaccinations, but there is also a large "gray zone" of pets that probably have intermediate protection and may or may not need repeat vaccination, depending on their risk of coming into contact with the disease.

These questions leave primary-care veterinarians in a very uncomfortable position, one that is not easy to resolve. Do they recommend annual vaccination in a manner that has demonstrated successful protection for decades, do they recommend skipping vaccines some years and hope that the protection lasts or do they measure blood tests (titers) and hope that the results are

# COMMON INFECTIOUS DISEASES

Let's discuss some of the diseases that create the need for vaccination in the first place. Following are the major canine infectious diseases and a simple explanation of each.

**Rabies:** A devastating viral disease that can be fatal in dogs and people. In fact, vaccination of dogs and cats is an important public-health measure to create a resistant animal buffer population to protect people from contracting the disease. Vaccination schedules are determined on a government level and are not optional for pet owners; rabies vaccination is required by law in all 50 states.

**Parvovirus:** A severe, potentially life-threatening disease that is easily transmitted between dogs. There are four strains of the virus, but it is believed that there is significant "cross-protection" between strains that may be included in individual vaccines.

**Distemper:** A potentially severe and life-threatening disease with a relatively high risk of exposure, especially in certain regions. In very high-risk distemper environments, young pups may be vaccinated with human measles vaccine, a related virus that offers cross-protection when administered at four to ten weeks of age.

**Hepatitis:** Caused by canine adenovirus type 1 (CAV-1), but since vaccination with the causative virus has a higher rate of adverse effects, cross-protection is derived from the use of adenovirus type 2 (CAV-2), a cause of respiratory disease and one of the potential causes of canine cough. Vaccination with CAV-2 provides long-term immunity against hepatitis, but relatively less protection against respiratory infection.

**Canine cough:** Also called tracheobronchitis, actually a fairly complicated result of viral and bacterial offenders; therefore, even with vaccination, protection is incomplete. Wherever dogs congregate, canine cough will likely be spread among them. Intranasal vaccination with *Bordetella* and parainfluenza is the best safeguard, but the duration of immunity does not appear to be very long, typically a year at most. These are non-core vaccines, but vaccination is sometimes mandated by boarding kennels, obedience classes, dog shows and other places where dogs congregate to try to minimize spread of infection.

**Leptospirosis:** A potentially fatal disease that is more common in some geographic regions. It is capable of being spread to humans. The disease varies with the individual "serovar," or strain, of *Leptospira* involved. Since there does not appear to be much cross-protection between serovars, protection is only as good as the likelihood that the serovar in the vaccine is the same as the one in the pet's local environment. Problems with *Leptospira* vaccines are that protection does not last very long, side effects are not uncommon and a large percentage of dogs (perhaps 30%) may not respond to vaccination.

***Borrelia burgdorferi:*** The cause of Lyme disease, the risk of which varies with the geographic area in which the pet lives and travels. Lyme disease is spread by deer ticks in the eastern US and western black-legged ticks in the western part of the country, and the risk of exposure is high in some regions. Lameness, fever and inappetence are most commonly seen in affected dogs. The extent of protection from the vaccine has not been conclusively demonstrated.

**Coronavirus:** This disease has a high risk of exposure, especially in areas where dogs congregate, but it typically causes only mild to moderate digestive upset (diarrhea, vomiting, etc.). Vaccines are available, but the duration of protection is believed to be relatively short and the effectiveness of the vaccine in preventing infection is considered low.

There are many other vaccinations available, including those for *Giardia* and canine adenovirus-1. While there may be some specific indications for their use, and local risk factors to be considered, they are not widely recommended for most dogs.

convincing enough to clearly indicate whether repeat vaccination is warranted?

Clearly, there are many more questions than there are answers. The important thing, as a pet owner, is to be aware of the issues and be able to work with your veterinarian to make decisions that are right for your pet. Be an informed consumer and you will appreciate the deliberation required in tailoring a vaccination program to best meet the needs of your pet. Expect also that this is an ongoing, ever-changing topic of debate; thus, the decisions you make this year won't necessarily be the same as the ones you make next year.

## NEUTERING/SPAYING

Sterilization procedures (neutering for males/spaying for females) are meant to accomplish several purposes. While the underlying premise is to address the risk of pet overpopulation, there are also some medical and behavioral benefits to the surgeries as well. For females, spaying prior to the first estrus (heat cycle) leads to a marked reduction in the risk of mammary cancer. There also will be no manifestations of "heat" to attract male dogs and no bleeding in the house. For males, there is prevention of testicular cancer and a reduction in the risk of prostate

> **SPAY'S THE WAY**
> Although spaying a female dog qualifies as major surgery—an ovariohysterectomy, in fact—this procedure is regarded as routine when performed by a qualified veterinarian on a healthy dog. The advantages to spaying a bitch are many and great. Spayed dogs do not develop uterine cancer or any life-threatening diseases of the genitals. Likewise, spayed dogs are at a significantly reduced risk of breast cancer. Bitches (and owners) are relieved of the demands of heat cycles. A spayed bitch will not leave bloody stains on your furniture during estrus, and you will not have to contend with single-minded macho males trying to climb your fence in order to seduce her. The spayed bitch's coat will not show the ill effects of her estrogen level's climbing such as a dull, lackluster outer coat or patches of hairlessness.

problems. In both sexes there may be some limited reduction in aggressive behaviors toward other dogs, and some diminishing of urine marking, roaming and mounting.

While neutering and spaying do indeed prevent animals from contributing to pet overpopulation, even no-cost and low-cost neutering options have not eliminated the problem. Perhaps one of the main reasons for this is that individuals who intentionally breed their dogs and those who allow their animals to run at large are the main causes of unwanted offspring. Also, animals in shelters are often there because they were abandoned or relinquished, not because they came from unplanned matings. Neutering/spaying is important, but it should be considered in the context of the real causes of animals' ending up in shelters and eventually being euthanized.

One of the important considerations regarding neutering is that it is a surgical procedure. This sometimes gets lost in discussions of low-cost procedures and commoditization of the process. In females, spaying is specifically referred to as an ovariohysterectomy. In this procedure, a midline incision is made in the abdomen and the entire uterus and both ovaries are surgically removed. While this is a major invasive surgical procedure, it usually has few complications, because it is typically performed on healthy young animals. However, it is major surgery, as any woman who has had a hysterectomy will attest.

In males, neutering has traditionally referred to castration, which involves the surgical removal of both testicles. While still a significant piece of surgery, there is not the abdominal exposure that is required in the female surgery. In addition, there is now a chemical sterilization option, in which a solution is injected into each testicle, leading to atrophy of the sperm-producing cells. This can typically be done under sedation rather than full anesthesia. This is a relatively new approach, and there are no long-term clinical studies yet available.

Neutering/spaying is typically done around six months of age at most veterinary hospitals, although techniques have been pioneered to perform the procedures in animals as young as eight weeks of age. In general, the surgeries on the very young animals are done for the specific reason of sterilizing them before they go to their new homes. This is done in some shelter hospitals for assurance that the animals will definitely not produce any pups. Otherwise, these organizations need to rely on owners to comply with their wishes to have the animals "altered" at a later date, something that does not always happen.

There are some exciting immunocontraceptive "vaccines" currently under development, and there may be a time when contraception in pets will not require surgical procedures. We anxiously await these developments.

S. E. M. by Dr. Dennis Kunkel, University of Hawaii.

*A scanning electron micrograph of a dog flea, Ctenocephalides canis, on dog hair.*

## EXTERNAL PARASITES

### FLEAS

Fleas have been around for millions of years and, while we have better tools now for controlling them than at any time in the past, there still is little chance that they will end up on an endangered species list. Actually, they are very well adapted to living on our pets, and they continue to adapt as we make advances.

The female flea can consume 15 times her weight in blood during active reproduction and can lay as many as 40 eggs a day. These eggs are very resistant to the effects of insecticides. They hatch into larvae, which then mature and spin cocoons. The immature fleas reside in this pupal stage until the time is right for feeding. This pupal stage is also very resistant to the effects of insecticides, and pupae can last in the environment without feeding for many months. Newly emergent fleas are attracted to animals by the warmth of the animals' bodies, movement and exhaled carbon dioxide. However, when they first emerge from their cocoons, they orient towards light; thus when an animal passes between a flea and the light source, casting a shadow, the flea pounces and starts to feed. If the animal turns out to be a dog or cat, the reproductive cycle continues. If the flea lands on another type of animal, including a person, the flea will bite but will then look for a more appropriate host. An emerging adult flea can survive without feeding for up to 12 months but, once it tastes blood, it can survive off its host for only three to four days.

It was once thought that fleas spend most of their lives in the environment, but we now know that fleas won't willingly jump off a dog unless leaping to another dog or when physically removed by brushing, bathing or other manipulation. Flea eggs, on the other hand, are shiny and smooth, and they roll off the animal and into the environment. The eggs, larvae and pupae then exist in the environment, but once the adult finds a susceptible animal, it's home sweet home until the flea is forced to seek refuge elsewhere.

Since adult fleas live on the animal and immature forms survive in the environment, a successful treatment plan must address all stages of the flea life cycle. There are now several safe and effective flea-control products that can be applied on a monthly basis. These include fipronil,

**FLEA PREVENTION FOR YOUR DOG**
- Discuss with your veterinarian the safest product to protect your dog, likely in the form of a monthly tablet or a liquid preparation placed on the back of the dog's neck.
- For dogs suffering from flea-bite dermatitis, a shampoo or topical insecticide treatment is required.
- Your lawn and property should be sprayed with an insecticide designed to kill fleas and ticks that lurk outdoors.
- Using a flea comb, check the dog's coat regularly for any signs of parasites.
- Practice good housekeeping. Vacuum floors, carpets and furniture regularly, especially in the areas that the dog frequents, and wash the dog's bedding weekly.
- Follow up house-cleaning with carpet shampoos and sprays to rid the house of fleas at all stages of development. Insect growth regulators are the safest option.

imidacloprid, selamectin and permethrin (found in several formulations). Most of these products have significant flea-killing rates within 24 hours. However, none of them will control the immature forms in the environment. To accomplish this, there are a variety of insect growth regulators that can be

## THE FLEA'S LIFE CYCLE

**Egg**

What came first, the flea or the egg? This age-old mystery is more difficult to comprehend than the actual cycle of the flea. Fleas usually live only about four months. A female can lay 2,000 eggs in her lifetime.

*Photo by Carolina Biological Supply Co.*

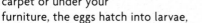

**Larva**

After ten days of rolling around your carpet or under your furniture, the eggs hatch into larvae, which feed on various and sundry debris. In days or months, depending on the climate, the larvae spin cocoons and develop into the pupal or nymph stage, which quickly develop into fleas.

**Pupa**

These immature fleas must locate a host within 10 to 14 days or they will die. Only about 1% of the flea population exist as adult fleas, while the other 99% exist as eggs, larvae or pupae.

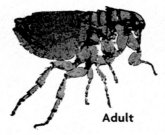

**Adult**

## KILL FLEAS THE NATURAL WAY

If you choose not to go the route of conventional medication, there are some natural ways to ward off fleas:

- Dust your dog with a natural flea powder, composed of such herbal goodies as rosemary, wormwood, pennyroyal, citronella, rue, tobacco powder and eucalyptus.
- Apply diatomaceous earth, the fossilized remains of single-cell algae, to your carpets, furniture and pet's bedding. Even though it's not good for dogs, it's even worse for fleas, which will dry up swiftly and die.
- Brush your dog frequently, give him adequate exercise and let him fast occasionally. All of these activities strengthen the dog's system and make him more resistant to disease and parasites.
- Bathe your dog with a capful of pennyroyal or eucalyptus oil.
- Feed a natural diet, free of additives and preservatives. Add some fresh garlic and brewer's yeast to the dog's morning portion, as these items have flea-repelling properties.

sprayed into the environment (e.g., pyriproxyfen, methoprene, fenoxycarb) as well as insect development inhibitors such as lufenuron that can be administered. These compounds have no effect on adult fleas, but they stop immature forms from developing into adults. In years gone by we relied heavily on toxic insecticides (such as organophosphates, organochlorines and carbamates) to manage the flea problem, but today's options are not only much safer to use on our pets but also safer for the environment.

## TICKS

Ticks are members of the spider class (arachnids) and are blood-sucking parasites capable of transmitting a variety of diseases, including Lyme disease, ehrlichiosis, babesiosis and Rocky Mountain spotted fever. It's easy to see ticks on your own skin, but it is more of a challenge when your dog is affected. Whenever you happen to be planning a stroll in a tick-infested area (especially forests, grassy or wooded areas or parks) be prepared to do a thorough inspection of your dog afterward to search for ticks. Ticks can be tricky, so make sure you spend time looking in the ears, between the toes and everywhere else where a tick might hide. Ticks need to be attached for 24–72 hours before they transmit most of the diseases that they carry, so you do have a window of opportunity for some preventive intervention.

Female ticks live to eat and

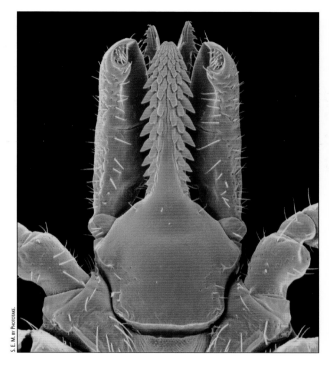

S. E. M. BY PHOTOTAKE.

A scanning electron micrograph of the head of a female deer tick, *Ixodes dammini*, a parasitic tick that carries Lyme disease.

### A TICKING BOMB

There is nothing good about a tick's harpooning his nose into your dog's skin. Among the diseases caused by ticks are Rocky Mountain spotted fever, canine ehrlichiosis, canine babesiosis, canine hepatozoonosis and Lyme disease. If a dog is allergic to the saliva of a female wood tick, he can develop tick paralysis.

breed. They can lay between 4,000 and 5,000 eggs and they die soon after. Males, on the other hand, live only to mate with the females and continue the process as long as they are able. Most ticks live on multiple hosts before parasitizing dogs. The immature forms typically reside on grass and shrubs, waiting for susceptible animals to walk by. The larvae and nymph stages typically feed on wildlife.

If only a few ticks are present on a dog, they can be plucked out, but it is important to remove the entire head and mouthparts, which may be deeply embedded

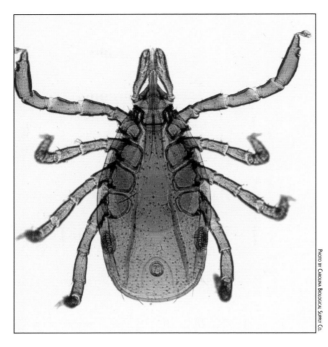

Photo by Carolina Biological Supply Co.

**Deer tick,**
**Ixodes dammini.**

in the skin. This is best accomplished with forceps designed especially for this purpose; fingers can be used but should be protected with rubber gloves, plastic wrap or at least a paper towel. The tick should be grasped as closely as possible to the animal's skin and should be pulled upward with steady, even pressure. Do not squeeze, crush or puncture the body of the tick or you risk exposure to any disease carried by that tick. Once the ticks have been removed, the sites of attachment should be disinfected. Your hands should then be washed with soap and water to further minimize risk of

contagion. The tick should be disposed of in a container of alcohol or household bleach.

Some of the newer flea products, specifically those with fipronil, selamectin and permethrin, have effect against some, but not all, species of tick. Flea collars containing appropriate pesticides (e.g., propoxur, chlorfenvinphos) can aid in tick control. In most areas, such collars should be placed on animals in March, at the beginning of the tick season, and changed regularly. Leaving the collar on when the pesticide level is waning invites the development of resistance. Amitraz collars are also good for tick control, and the active ingredient does not interfere with other flea-control products. The ingredient helps prevent the attachment of ticks to the skin and will cause those ticks already on the skin to detach themselves.

### TICK CONTROL

Removal of underbrush and leaf litter and the thinning of trees in areas where tick control is desired are recommended. These actions remove the cover and food sources for small animals that serve as hosts for ticks. With continued mowing of grasses in these areas, the probability of ticks' surviving is further reduced. A variety of insecticide ingredients (e.g., resmethrin, carbaryl, permethrin, chlorpyrifos, dioxathion and allethrin) are registered for tick control around the home.

### MITES

Mites are tiny arachnid parasites that parasitize the skin of dogs. Skin diseases caused by mites are referred to as "mange," and there are many different forms seen in dogs. These forms are very different from one another, each one warranting an individual description.

Sarcoptic mange, or scabies, is one of the itchiest conditions that affects dogs. The microscopic *Sarcoptes* mites burrow into the superficial layers of the skin and can drive dogs crazy with itchiness. They are also communicable to people, although they can't complete their reproductive cycle on people. In addition to being tiny, the mites also are often difficult to find when trying to make a diagnosis. Skin scrapings from multiple areas are examined microscopically but, even then, sometimes the mites cannot be found.

Fortunately, scabies is relatively easy to treat, and there are a variety of products that will successfully kill the mites. Since the mites can't live in the environment for very long without feeding, a complete cure is usually possible within four to eight weeks.

Cheyletiellosis is caused by a relatively large mite, which sometimes can be seen even without a microscope. Often referred to as "walking dandruff," this also causes itching, but not usually as profound as with scabies.

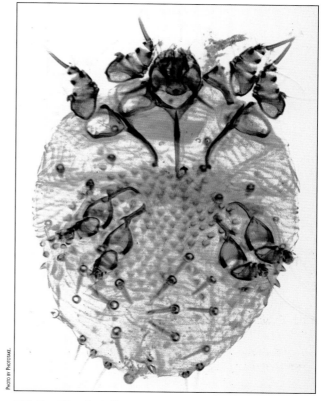

PHOTO BY PHOTOTAKE.

*Sarcoptes scabiei, commonly known as the "itch mite."*

While *Cheyletiella* mites can survive somewhat longer in the environment than scabies mites, they too are relatively easy to treat, being responsive to not only the medications used to treat scabies but also often to flea-control products.

*Otodectes cynotis* is the canine ear mite and is one of the more common causes of mange, especially in young dogs in shelters or pet stores. That's because the mites are typically present in large numbers and are quickly spread to

Micrograph of a dog louse, *Heterodoxus spiniger*. Female lice attach their eggs to the hairs of the dog. As the eggs hatch, the larval lice bite and feed on the blood. Lice can also feed on dead skin and hair. This feeding activity can cause hair loss and skin problems.

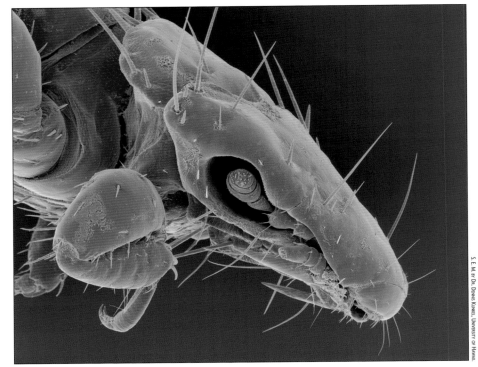

S. E. M. by Dr. Dennis Kunkel, University of Hawaii.

nearby animals. The mites rarely do much harm but can be difficult to eradicate if the treatment regimen is not comprehensive. While many try to treat the condition with ear drops only, this is the most common cause of treatment failure. Ear drops cause the mites to simply move out of the ears and as far away as possible (usually to the base of the tail) until the insecticide levels in the ears drop to an acceptable level—then it's back to business as usual! The successful treatment of ear mites requires treating all animals in the household with a systemic insecticide, such as selamectin, or a combination of miticidal ear drops combined with whole-body flea-control preparations.

Demodicosis, sometimes referred to as red mange, can be one of the most difficult forms of mange to treat. Part of the problem has to do with the fact that the mites live in the hair follicles and they are relatively well shielded from topical and systemic products. The main issue, however, is that demodectic mange typically results only when there is some underlying process interfering with the dog's immune system.

Since *Demodex* mites are

normal residents of the skin of mammals, including humans, there is usually a mite population explosion only when the immune system fails to keep the number of mites in check. In young animals, the immune deficit may be transient or may reflect an actual inherited immune problem. In older animals, demodicosis is usually seen only when there is another disease hampering the immune system, such as diabetes, cancer, thyroid problems or the use of immune-suppressing drugs. Accordingly, treatment involves not only trying to kill the mange mites but also discerning what is interfering with immune function and correcting it if possible.

Chiggers represent several different species of mite that don't parasitize dogs specifically, but do latch on to passersby and can cause irritation. The problem is most prevalent in wooded areas in the late summer and fall. Treatment is not difficult, as the mites do not complete their life cycle on dogs and are susceptible to a variety of miticidal products.

### MOSQUITOES

Mosquitoes have long been known to transmit a variety of diseases to people, as well as just being biting pests during warm weather. They also pose a real risk to pets. Not only do they carry deadly heartworms but recently there also has been much concern over their involvement with West Nile virus. While we can avoid heartworm with the use of preventive medications, there are no such preventives for West Nile virus. The only method of prevention in endemic areas is active mosquito control. Fortunately, most dogs that have been exposed to the virus only developed flu-like symptoms and, to date, there have not been the large number of reported deaths in canines as seen in some other species.

ILLUSTRATION BY PHOTODAKE

**Illustration of Demodex folliculoram.**

## MOSQUITO REPELLENT

Low concentrations of DEET (less than 10%), found in many human mosquito repellents, have been safely used in dogs but, in these concentrations, probably give only about two hours of protection. DEET may be safe in these small concentrations, but since it is not licensed for use on dogs, there is no research proving its safety for dogs. Products containing permethrin give the longest-lasting protection, perhaps two to four weeks. As DEET is not licensed for use on dogs, and both DEET and permethrin can be quite toxic to cats, appropriate care should be exercised. Other products, such as those containing oil of citronella, also have some mosquito-repellent activity, but typically have a relatively short duration of action.

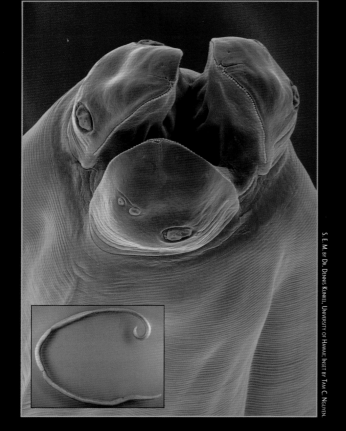

S. E. M. BY DR. DENNIS KUNKEL, UNIVERSITY OF HAWAII. INSET BY TAM C. NGUYEN

The ascarid roundworm *Toxocara canis*, showing the mouth with three lips. INSET: Photomicrograph of the roundworm *Ascaris lumbricoides*.

## INTERNAL PARASITES: WORMS

### ASCARIDS

Ascarids are intestinal roundworms that rarely cause severe disease in dogs. Nonetheless, they are of major public health significance because they can be transferred to people. Sadly, it is children who are most commonly affected by the parasite, probably from inadvertently ingesting ascarid-contaminated soil. In fact, many yards and children's sandboxes contain appreciable numbers of ascarid eggs. So, while ascarids don't bite dogs or latch onto their intestines to suck blood, they do cause some nasty medical conditions in children and are best eradicated from our furry friends. Because pups can start passing ascarid eggs by three weeks of age, most parasite-control programs begin at two to three weeks of age and are repeated every two weeks until pups are eight weeks old. It is important to realize

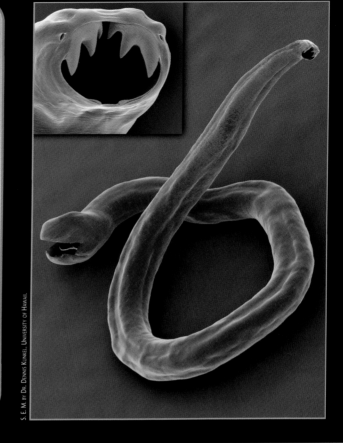

S. E. M. BY DR. DENNIS KUNKEL, UNIVERSITY OF HAWAII.

that bitches can pass ascarids to their pups even if they test negative prior to whelping. Accordingly, bitches are best treated at the same time as the pups.

### HOOKWORMS

Unlike ascarids, hookworms do latch onto a dog's intestinal tract and can cause significant loss of blood and protein. Similar to ascarids, hookworms can be transmitted to humans, where they cause a condition known as cutaneous larval migrans. Dogs can become infected either by consuming the infective larvae or by the larvae's penetrating the skin directly. People most often get infected when they are lying on the ground (such as on a beach) and the larvae penetrate the skin. Yes, the larvae can penetrate through a beach blanket. Hookworms are typically susceptible to the same medications used to treat ascarids.

**The hookworm *Ancylostoma caninum* infests the intestines of dogs. INSET: Note the row of hooks at the posterior end, used to anchor the worm to the intestinal wall.**

### WHIPWORMS

Whipworms latch onto the lower aspects of the dog's colon and can cause cramping and diarrhea. Eggs do not start to appear in the dog's feces until about three months after the dog was infected. This worm has a peculiar life cycle, which makes it more difficult to control than ascarids or hookworms. The good thing is that whipworms rarely are transferred to people.

Some of the medications used to treat ascarids and hookworms are also effective against whipworms, but, in general, a separate treatment protocol is needed. Since most of the medications are effective against the adults but not the eggs or larvae, treatment is typically repeated in three weeks, and then often in three

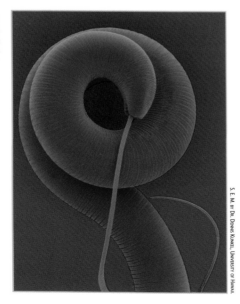

**Adult whipworm, *Trichuris* sp., an intestinal parasite.**

S. E. M. BY DR. DENNIS KUNKEL, UNIVERSITY OF HAWAII.

> ## WORM-CONTROL GUIDELINES
> • Practice sanitary habits with your dog and home.
> • Clean up after your dog and don't let him sniff or eat other dogs' droppings.
> • Control insects and fleas in the dog's environment. Fleas, lice, cockroaches, beetles, mice and rats can act as hosts for various worms.
> • Prevent dogs from eating uncooked meat, raw poultry and dead animals.
> • Keep dogs and children from playing in sand and soil.
> • Kennel dogs on cement or gravel; avoid dirt runs.
> • Administer heartworm preventives regularly.
> • Have your vet examine your dog's stools at your annual visits.
> • Select a boarding kennel carefully so as to avoid contamination from other dogs or an unsanitary environment.
> • Prevent dogs from roaming. Obey local leash laws.

months as well. Unfortunately, since dogs don't develop resistance to whipworms, it is difficult to prevent them from getting reinfected if they visit soil contaminated with whipworm eggs.

### TAPEWORMS

There are many different species of tapeworm that affect dogs, but *Dipylidium caninum* is probably the most common and is spread by fleas. Flea larvae feed on organic debris and tapeworm eggs in the environment and, when a dog chews at himself and manages to ingest fleas, he might get a dose of tapeworm at the same time. The tapeworm then develops further in the intestine of the dog.

The tapeworm itself, which is a parasitic flatworm that latches onto the intestinal wall, is composed of numerous segments. When the segments break off into the intestine (as proglottids), they may accumulate around the rectum, like grains of rice. While this tapeworm is disgusting in its behavior, it is not directly communicable to humans (although humans can also get infected by swallowing fleas).

A much more dangerous flatworm is *Echinococcus multilocularis*, which is typically found in foxes, coyotes and wolves. The eggs are passed in the feces and infect rodents, and, when dogs eat the rodents, the dogs can be infected by thousands of adult tapeworms. While the parasites don't cause many problems in dogs, this is considered the most lethal worm infection that people can get. Take appropriate precautions if you live in an area in which these tapeworms are found. Do not use mulch that may contain feces of dogs, cats or wildlife, and

discourage your pets from hunting wildlife. Treat these tapeworm infections aggressively in pets, because if humans get infected, approximately half die.

### HEARTWORMS

Heartworm disease is caused by the parasite *Dirofilaria immitis* and is seen in dogs around the world. A member of the roundworm group, it is spread between dogs by the bite of an infected mosquito. The mosquito injects infective larvae into the dog's skin with its bite, and these larvae develop under the skin for a period of time before making their way to the heart. There they develop into adults, which grow and create blockages of the heart, lungs and major blood vessels there. They also start producing offspring (microfilariae)

A dog tapeworm proglottid (body segment).

S. E. M. BY DR. DENNIS KUNKEL, UNIVERSITY OF HAWAII.

The dog tapeworm *Taenia pisiformis*.

S. E. M. BY DR. DENNIS KUNKEL, UNIVERSITY OF HAWAII.

## A Look at Internal Parasites

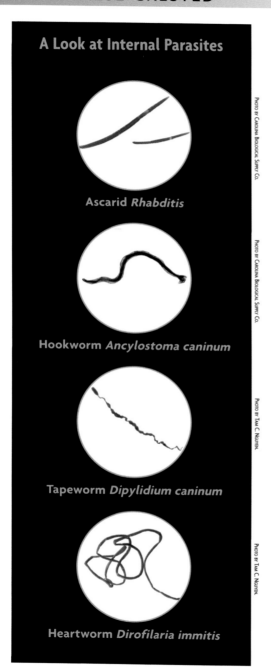

Ascarid *Rhabditis*

PHOTO BY CAROLINA BIOLOGICAL SUPPLY CO.

Hookworm *Ancylostoma caninum*

PHOTO BY CAROLINA BIOLOGICAL SUPPLY CO.

Tapeworm *Dipylidium caninum*

PHOTO BY TAM C. NGUYEN.

Heartworm *Dirofilaria immitis*

PHOTO BY TAM C. NGUYEN.

and these microfilariae circulate in the bloodstream, waiting to hitch a ride when the next mosquito bites. Once in the mosquito, the microfilariae develop into infective larvae and the entire process is repeated.

When dogs get infected with heartworm, over time they tend to develop symptoms associated with heart disease, such as coughing, exercise intolerance and potentially many other manifestations. Diagnosis is confirmed by either seeing the microfilariae themselves in blood samples or using immunologic tests (antigen testing) to identify the presence of adult heartworms. Since antigen tests measure the presence of adult heartworms and microfilarial tests measure offspring produced by adults, neither are positive until six to seven months after the initial infection. However, the beginning of damage can occur by fifth-stage larvae as early as three months after infection. Thus it is possible for dogs to be harboring problem-causing larvae for up to three months before either type of test would identify an infection.

The good news is that there are great protocols available for preventing heartworm in dogs. Testing is critical in the process, and it is important to understand the benefits as well as the limitations of such testing. All dogs six months of age or older that have not been on continuous heartworm-preventive medication should be

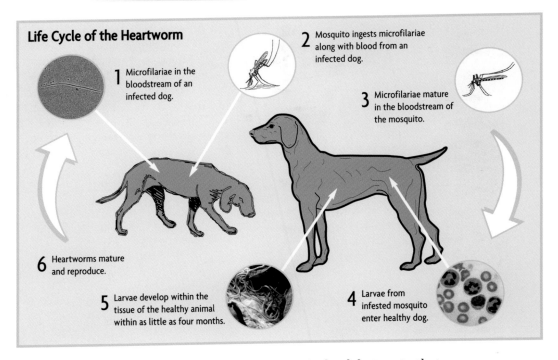

**Life Cycle of the Heartworm**

**1** Microfilariae in the bloodstream of an infected dog.

**2** Mosquito ingests microfilariae along with blood from an infected dog.

**3** Microfilariae mature in the bloodstream of the mosquito.

**4** Larvae from infested mosquito enter healthy dog.

**5** Larvae develop within the tissue of the healthy animal within as little as four months.

**6** Heartworms mature and reproduce.

screened with microfilarial or antigen tests. For dogs receiving preventive medication, periodic antigen testing helps assess the effectiveness of the preventives. The American Heartworm Society guidelines suggest that annual retesting may not be necessary when owners have absolutely provided continuous heartworm prevention. Retesting on a two- to three-year interval may be sufficient in these cases. However, your veterinarian will likely have specific guidelines under which heartworm preventives will be prescribed, and many prefer to err on the side of safety and retest annually.

It is indeed fortunate that heartworm is relatively easy to prevent, because treatments can be as life-threatening as the disease itself. Treatment requires a two-step process that kills the adult heartworms first and then the microfilariae. Prevention is obviously preferable; this involves a once-monthly oral or topical treatment. The most common oral preventives include ivermectin (not suitable for some breeds), moxidectin and milbemycin oxime; the once-a-month topical drug selamectin provides heartworm protection in addition to flea, tick and other parasite controls.

# CHINESE CRESTED

When we bring home a puppy, full of the energy and exuberance that accompanies youth, we hope for a long, happy and fulfilling relationship with the new family member. Even when we adopt an older dog, we look forward to the years of companionship ahead with a new canine friend. However, aging is inevitable for all creatures, and there will come a time when your Chinese Crested reaches his senior years and will need special considerations and attention to his care.

### WHEN IS MY DOG A "SENIOR"?

In general, purebred dogs are considered to have achieved senior status when they reach 75% of their breed's average lifespan, with lifespan being based on breed size. Your Chinese Crested has an average lifespan of about 13 years and thus is a senior citizen at around 10 years of age.

Obviously, the old "seven dog years to one human year" theory is not exact. In puppyhood, a dog's year is actually comparable to more than seven human years, considering the puppy's rapid growth during his first year. Then, in adulthood, the ratio decreases.

> **WHAT A RELIEF!**
> Much like young puppies, older dogs do not have as much control over their excretory functions as they do as non-seniors. Their muscle control fades and, as such, they cannot "hold it" for as long as they used to. This is easily remedied by additional trips outside. If your dog's sight is failing, have the yard well lit at night and/or lead him to his relief site on lead. Incontinence should be discussed with your vet.

Regardless, the more viable rule of thumb is that the larger the dog, the shorter his expected lifespan. Of course, this can vary among individual dogs, with many living longer than expected, which we hope is the case!

### WHAT ARE THE SIGNS OF AGING?

By the time your dog has reached his senior years, you will know him very well, so the physical and behavioral changes that accompany aging should be noticeable to you. Humans and dogs share the most obvious

# CANINE COGNITIVE DYSFUNCTION

## "OLD-DOG" SYNDROME

There are many ways for you to evaluate "old-dog" syndrome. Veterinarians have defined canine cognitive dysfunction as the gradual deterioration of cognitive abilities, indicated by changes in the dog's behavior. When a dog changes his routine response, and maladies have been eliminated as the cause of these behavioral changes, then canine cognitive dysfunction is the usual diagnosis.

More than half the dogs over eight years old suffer from some form of this syndrome. The older the dog, the more chance he has of suffering from it. In humans, doctors often dismiss the canine cognitive dysfunction behavioral changes as part of "winding down."

There are four major signs of canine cognitive dysfunction: frequent potty accidents inside the home, sleeping much more or much less than normal, acting confused and failing to respond to social stimuli.

## SYMPTOMS

### CONFUSION
- Goes outside and just stands there.
- Appears confused with a faraway look in his eyes.
- Hides more often.
- Doesn't recognize friends.
- Doesn't come when called.
- Walks around listlessly and without a destination.

### SLEEP PATTERNS
- Awakens more slowly.
- Sleeps more than normal during the day.
- Sleeps less during the night.

### CONFUSION
- Goes outside and just stands there.
- Appears confused with a faraway look in his eyes.
- Hides more often.
- Doesn't recognize friends.
- Doesn't come when called.
- Walks around listlessly and without a destination.

### SLEEP PATTERNS
- Awakens more slowly.
- Sleeps more than normal during the day.
- Sleeps less during the night.

physical sign of aging: gray hair! Graying often occurs first on the muzzle and face, around the eyes. Other telltale signs are the dog's overall decrease in activity. Your older dog might be more content to nap and rest, and he may not show the same old enthusiasm when it's time to play in the yard or go for a walk. Other physical signs include significant weight loss or gain; more labored movement; skin and coat problems, possibly hair loss; sight and/or hearing problems; changes in toileting habits, perhaps seeming "unhousebroken" at times; tooth decay, bad breath or other mouth problems.

There are behavioral changes that go along with aging, too.

There are numerous causes for behavioral changes. Sometimes a dog's apparent confusion results from a physical change like diminished sight or hearing. If his confusion causes him to be afraid, he may act aggressively or defensively. He may sleep more frequently because his daily walks, though shorter now, tire him out. He may begin to experience separation anxiety or, conversely, become less interested in petting and attention.

There also are clinical conditions that cause behavioral changes in older dogs. One such condition is known as canine cognitive dysfunction (familiarly known as "old-dog" syndrome). It can be frustrating for an owner

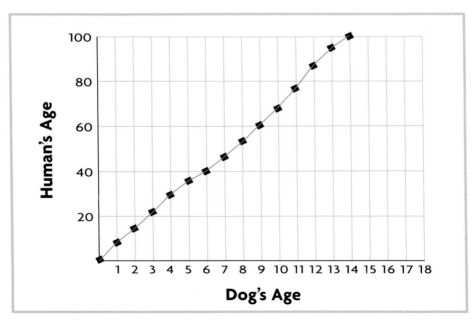

whose dog is affected with cognitive dysfunction, as it can result in behavioral changes of all types, most seemingly unexplainable. Common changes include the dog's forgetting aspects of the daily routine, such as times to eat, go out for walks, relieve himself and the like. Along the same lines, you may take your dog out at the regular time for a potty trip and he may have no idea why he is there. Sometimes a placid dog will begin to show aggressive or possessive tendencies or, conversely, a hyperactive dog will start to "mellow out."

Disease also can be the cause of behavioral changes in senior dogs. Hormonal problems (Cushing's disease is common in older dogs), diabetes and thyroid disease can cause increased appetite, which can lead to aggression related to food guarding. It's better to be proactive with your senior dog, making more frequent trips to the vet if necessary and having bloodwork done to test for the diseases that can commonly befall older dogs.

This is not to say that, as dogs age, they all fall apart physically and become nasty in personality. The aforementioned changes are discussed to alert owners to the things that may happen as their dogs get older. Many hardy dogs remain active and alert well into old age. However, it can be

**WEATHER WORRIES**

Older pets are less tolerant of extremes in weather, both heat and cold. Your older dog should not spend extended periods in the sun; when outdoors in the warm weather, make sure he does not become overheated. In chilly weather, consider a non-woolen sweater for your dog when outdoors and limit time spent outside. Whether or not his coat is thinning, he will need provisions to keep him warm when the weather is cold. You may even place his bed by a heating duct in your living room or bedroom.

frustrating and heartbreaking for owners to see their beloved dogs change physically and temperamentally. Just know that it's the same Chinese Crested under there, and that he still loves you and appreciates your care, which he needs now more than ever.

## HOW DO I CARE FOR MY AGING DOG?

Again, every dog is an individual in terms of aging. Your dog might reach the estimated "senior" age for Cresteds and show no signs of slowing down. However, even if he shows no outward signs of aging, he should begin a senior-care program once he reaches the determined age. He may not show it, but he's not a pup anymore! By providing him with extra

Even the senior dog shouldn't be allowed to choose his own television and video programs—unless, of course, he knows how to operate the remotes.

attention to his veterinary care at this age, you will be practicing good preventive medicine, ensuring that the rest of your dog's life will be as long, active, happy and healthy as possible. If you do notice indications of aging, such as graying and/or changes in sleeping, eating or toileting habits, this is a sign to set up a senior-care visit with your vet right away to make sure that these changes are not related to any health problems.

To start, senior dogs should visit the vet twice yearly for exams, routine tests and overall evaluations. Many veterinarians have special screening programs especially for senior dogs that can include a thorough physical exam; blood test to determine complete blood count; serum biochemistry test, which screens for liver, kidney and blood problems as well as cancer; urinalysis; and dental exams. With these tests, it can be determined whether your dog has any health problems; the results also establish a baseline for your pet against which future test results can be compared.

In addition to these tests, your vet may suggest additional testing, including an EKG, tests for glaucoma and other problems of the eye, chest X-rays, screening for tumors, blood pressure test, test for thyroid function and screening for parasites and reassessment of his preventive program. Your vet also will ask you questions about your dog's diet and activity level, what you feed and the amounts that you feed. This information, along with his evaluation of the dog's overall condition, will enable him to suggest proper dietary changes, if needed.

This may seem like quite a work-up for your pet, but veterinarians advise that older dogs need more frequent attention so that any health problems can be detected as early as possible. Serious conditions like kidney disease, heart disease and cancer may not present outward symptoms, or the problem may go undetected if the symptoms are mistaken by owners as just part of the aging process.

There are some conditions more common in elderly dogs that are difficult to ignore. Cognitive dysfunction shares much in common with senility and Alzheimer's disease, and dogs are not immune. Dogs can become confused and/or disoriented, lose their house-training, have abnormal sleep-wake cycles and interact differently with their owners. Be heartened by the fact that, in some ways, there are more treatment options for dogs with cognitive dysfunction than for people with similar conditions. There is good evidence that continued stimulation in the form of games, play, training and exercise can help to maintain cognitive function. There are also medications (such as seligiline) and antioxidant-fortified senior diets that have been shown to be beneficial.

Cancer is also a condition more common in the elderly. Almost all of the cancers seen in people are also seen in pets. While we can't control the effects of second-hand smoke, lung cancer, which is a major killer in humans, is relatively rare in dogs. If pets are getting regular physical examinations, cancers are often detected early. There are a variety of cancer therapies available today, and many pets continue to live happy lives with appropriate treatment.

Degenerative joint disease, often referred to as arthritis, is another malady common to both elderly dogs and humans. A lifetime of wear and tear on joints and running around at play eventually take toll and result in stiffness and difficulty in getting around. As dogs live longer and healthier lives, it is natural that they should eventually feel some of the effects of aging. Once again, if regular veterinary care has been available, your pet was not carrying extra pounds all those years and wearing those joints out before their time. If your pet was unfortunate enough to inherit hip dysplasia, osteochondrosis dissecans, or any of the other

## ACCIDENT ALERT!

Just as we puppy-proof our homes for the new member of the family, we must accident-proof our homes for the older dog. You want to create a safe environment in which the senior dog can get around easily and comfortably, with no dangers. A dog that slips and falls in old age is much more prone to injury than an adult, making accident prevention even more important. Likewise, dogs are more prone to falls in old age, as they do not have the same balance and coordination that they once had. Throw rugs on hardwood floors are slippery and pose a risk; even a throw rug on a carpeted surface can be an obstacle for the senior dog. Consider putting down non-slip surfaces or confining your dog to carpeted rooms only.

developmental orthopedic diseases, battling the onset of degenerative joint disease was probably a longstanding goal. In any case, there are now many effective remedies for managing degenerative joint disease and a number of remarkable surgeries as well.

Aside from the extra veterinary care, there is much you can do at home to keep your older dog in good condition. The dog's diet is an important factor. If your dog's appetite decreases, he will not be getting the nutrients he needs. He also will lose weight, which is unhealthy for a dog at a proper weight. Conversely, an older dog's metabolism is slower and he usually exercises less, but he should not be allowed to become obese. Obesity in an older dog is especially risky, because extra pounds mean extra stress on the body, increasing his vulnerability to heart disease. Additionally, the extra pounds make it harder for the dog to move about.

You should discuss age-related feeding changes with your vet. For a dog who has lost interest in food, it may be suggested to try some different types of food until you find something new that the dog likes. For an obese dog, a "light" formula dog food or reducing food portions may be advised, along with exercise appropriate to his physical condition and energy level.

As for exercise, the senior dog should not be allowed to become a "couch potato" despite his old age. He may not be able to handle the morning run, long walks and vigorous games of fetch, but he still needs to get up and get moving. Keep up with your daily walks, but keep the distances shorter and let your dog set the pace. If he gets to the point where he's not up for walks, let him stroll around the yard. On the

## RUBDOWN REMEDY

A good remedy for an aching dog is to give him a gentle massage each day, or even a few times a day if possible. This can be especially beneficial before your dog gets out of his bed in the morning. Just as in humans, massage can decrease pain in dogs, whether the dog is arthritic or just afflicted by the stiffness that accompanies old age. Gently massage his joints and limbs, as well as petting him on his entire body. This can help his circulation and flexibility and ease any joint or muscle aches. Massaging your dog has benefits for you, too; in fact, just petting our dogs can cause reduced levels of stress and lower our blood pressure. Massage and petting also help you find any previously undetected lumps, bumps or abnormalities. Often these are not visible and only turn up by being felt.

other hand, many dogs remain very active in their senior years, so base changes to the exercise program on your own individual dog and what he's capable of. Don't worry, your Chinese Crested will let you know when it's time to rest.

Keep up with your grooming routine as you always have. Be extra diligent about checking the skin and coat for problems. Older dogs can experience thinning coats as a normal aging process, but they can also lose hair as a result of medical problems. Some thinning is normal, but patches of baldness or the loss of significant amounts of hair is not.

Hopefully, you've been regular with brushing your dog's teeth throughout his life. Healthy teeth directly affect overall good health. We already know that bacteria from gum infections can enter the dog's body through the damaged gums and travel to the organs. At a stage in life when his organs don't function as well as they used to, you don't want anything to put additional strain on them. Clean teeth also contribute to a healthy immune system. Offering the dental-type chews in addition to toothbrushing can help, as they remove plaque and tartar as the dog chews.

Along with the same good care you've given him all of his life, pay a little extra attention to your dog in his senior years and

## CAUSES OF CHANGE

Cognitive dysfunction may not be the cause of all changes in your older dog; illness and medication can also affect him. Things like diabetes, Cushing's disease, cancer and brain tumors are serious physical problems but can cause behavioral changes as well. Older dogs are more prone to these conditions, which should not be overlooked as possibilities for your dog's acting not like his "old self." Any significant changes in your senior's behavior are good reasons to take your dog to the vet for a thorough exam.

Your dog's reactions to medication can cause changes as well. The various types of corticosteroids are often cited as affecting a dog's behavior. If your vet prescribes any type of drug, discuss possible side effects before administering the medication to your dog.

keep up with twice-yearly trips to the vet. The sooner a problem is uncovered, the greater the chances of a full recovery.

## SAYING GOODBYE

While you can help your dog live as long a life as possible, you can't help him live forever. A dog's lifespan is short when compared to that of a human, so it is inevitable that pet owners will experience loss. To many, losing a beloved dog is like losing a family member. Our dogs are part of our lives every day; they are our true loyal friends and always seem to know when it's time to comfort us, to celebrate with us or to just provide the company of a caring friend. Even whether we know that our dog is nearing his final days, we can never quite prepare for his being gone.

Many dogs live out long lives and simply die of old age. Others unfortunately are taken suddenly by illness or accident, and still others find their senior years compromised by disease and physical problems. In some of these cases, owners find themselves having to make difficult decisions.

Memorializing your pet in a cemetery has become a popular option for many dog owners.

OUR BABY
PEPPER FRIEDMAN
1976 — 1984

## PET LOSS AND CHILDREN

Everyone in the family will be affected by the death of a pet. Many children form strong bonds with their dogs, so losing a pet can be especially painful. For some children, losing a pet will be their first experience with the death of a loved one. This can present a difficult and awkward situation to parents, who must provide a delicate yet honest explanation appropriate to the ages of the children. Regardless of the child's age, he should be encouraged to talk about and express his feelings, and to ask questions. Providing explanations that the dog is "asleep" or has "gone away" may cause a child to think that the pet will return or that death is temporary, so euphemisms such as these may be best avoided. Children at different age levels will manifest grief in different ways. Younger children, say between two and six years of age, have less understanding of what death is, while older children, adolescents and teens grasp the concept and may manifest their grief more outwardly, possibly even experiencing denial. At any age, open discussions should be encouraged so that children can express their grief and concerns. Of course, children should be part of the decision about whether or not to get a new pet. Generally, the younger the child, the more readily he will accept a new pet into the family.

# SHOWING YOUR

# CHINESE CRESTED

Is dog showing in your blood? Are you excited by the idea of gaiting your handsome Chinese Crested around the ring to the thunderous applause of an enthusiastic audience? Are you certain that your beloved Chinese Crested is flawless? You are not alone! Every loving owner thinks that his dog has no faults, or too few to mention. No matter how many times an owner reads the breed standard, he cannot find any faults in his aristocratic companion dog. If this sounds like you, and if you are considering entering your Chinese Crested in a dog show, here are some basic questions to ask yourself:

- Did you purchase a "show-quality" puppy from the breeder?
- Is your puppy at least six months of age?
- Does the puppy exhibit correct show type for his breed?
- Does your puppy have any disqualifying faults?
- Is your Chinese Crested registered with the American Kennel Club?
- How much time do you have to devote to training, grooming,

conditioning and exhibiting your dog?
- Do you understand the rules and regulations of a dog show?
- Do you have time to learn how to show your dog properly?
- Do you have the financial resources to invest in showing your dog?
- Will you show the dog yourself

**MEET THE KENNEL CLUBS**

For reliable up-to-date information about registration, dog shows and other canine competitions, contact one of the national registries by mail or via the Internet.

American Kennel Club
5580 Centerview Dr., Raleigh, NC 27606-3390
www.akc.org

United Kennel Club
100 E. Kilgore Road, Kalamazoo, MI 49002
www.ukcdogs.com

Canadian Kennel Club
89 Skyway Ave., Suite 100, Etobicoke, Ontario
M9W 6R4 Canada
www.ckc.ca

The Kennel Club
1-5 Clarges St., Piccadilly, London W1Y 8AB, UK
www.the-kennel-club.org.uk

### DRESS THE PART

It's a dog show, so don't forget your costume. Even though the show is about the dog, you also must play your role well. You have been cast as the "dog handler" and you must smartly dress the part. Solid colors make a nice complement to the dog's coat, but choose colors that contrast. You don't want to be wearing a solid color that blends mostly or entirely with the major or only color of your dog. Whether the show is indoors or out, you still must dress properly. You want the judge to perceive you as being professional, so polish, polish, polish! And don't forget to wear sensible shoes; remember, you have to gait around the ring with your dog.

or hire a professional handler?
- Do you have a vehicle that can accommodate your weekend trips to the dog shows?

Success in the show ring requires more than a pretty face, a waggy tail and a pocketful of liver. Even though dog shows can be exciting and enjoyable, the sport of conformation makes great demands on the exhibitors and the dogs. Winning exhibitors live for their dogs, devoting time and money to their dogs' presentation, conditioning and training. Very few novices, even those with good dogs, will find themselves in the winners' circle, though it does happen. Don't be disheartened, though. Every exhibitor began as a novice and worked his way up to the Group ring. It's the "working your way up" part that you must keep in mind.

Assuming that you have purchased a puppy of the correct type and quality for showing, let's begin to examine the world of showing and what's required to get started. Although the entry fee into a dog show is nominal, there are lots of other hidden costs involved with "finishing" your Chinese Crested, that is, making him a champion. Things like equipment, travel, training and conditioning all cost money. A more serious campaign will include fees for a professional handler, boarding, cross-country travel and advertising. Top-winning show dogs can represent a very considerable investment—over $100,000 has been spent in campaigning some dogs. (The investment can be less, of course, for owners who don't use professional handlers.)

Many owners, on the other hand, enter their "average" Chinese Cresteds in dog shows for the fun and enjoyment of it. Dog showing makes an absorbing hobby, with many rewards for dogs and owners alike. If you're having fun, meeting other people who share your interests and enjoying the overall experience, you likely will catch the "bug." Once the dog-show bug bites, its effects can last a lifetime; it's certainly much better than a deer tick! Soon you will be envisioning yourself in the center ring at the Westminster Kennel Club Dog Show in New York City, competing for the prestigious Best in Show cup. This magical dog show is televised annually from Madison Square Garden, and the victorious dog becomes a celebrity overnight.

## AKC CONFORMATION SHOWING

### GETTING STARTED

Visiting a dog show as a spectator is a great place to start. Pick up the show catalog to find out what time your breed is being shown, who is judging the breed and in

Campaigned by Victor Helu, Ch. Gingery's Cheesecake did much to put the Powderpuff on the map! She was one of the top Chinese Crested Powderpuffs and was ranked #2 Chinese Crested in the US. The dam of 12 champions, she was the third Chinese Crested and first Powderpuff Dam of Distinction.

which ring the classes will be held. To start, Chinese Cresteds compete against other Chinese Cresteds, and the winner is selected as Best of Breed by the judge. This is the procedure for each breed. At a group show, all of the Best of Breed winners go on to compete for Group One in their respective group. For example, all Best of Breed winners in a given group compete against each other;

Ch. Jann's Kriquet Kolada, the oldest Crested to become an AKC champion, was a multiple Best in Show winner and was named "Chinese Crested of the Year" in 1988. Owner, Arleen Butterklee.

Each dog takes a turn around the ring as the judge evaluates the dog's movement.

this is done for all seven groups. Finally, all seven group winners go head to head in the ring for the Best in Show award.

What most spectators don't understand is the basic idea of conformation. A dog show is often referred as a "conformation" show. This means that the judge should decide how each dog stacks up (conforms) to the breed standard for his given breed: how well does this Chinese Crested conform to the ideal representative detailed in the standard? Ideally, this is what happens. In reality, however, this ideal often gets slighted as the judge compares Chinese Crested #1 to Chinese Crested #2. Again, the ideal is that each dog is judged based on his merits in comparison to his breed standard, not in comparison to the other dogs in the ring. It is easier for judges to compare dogs of the same breed to decide which they think is the better specimen; in the Group and Best in Show ring, however, it is very difficult to compare one breed to another, like apples to oranges. Thus the dog's conformation to the breed standard—not to mention advertising dollars and good handling—is essential to success in conformation shows. The dog described in the standard (the standard for each AKC breed is written and approved by the breed's national parent club and then submitted to the AKC for

approval) is the perfect dog of that breed, and breeders keep their eye on the standard when they choose which dogs to breed, hoping to get closer and closer to the ideal with each litter.

Another good first step for the novice is to join a dog club. You will be astonished by the many and different kinds of dog clubs in the country, with about 5,000 clubs holding events every year. Most clubs require that prospective new members present two letters of recommendation from existing members. Perhaps you've made some friends visiting a show held by a particular club and you would like to join that club. Dog clubs may specialize in a single breed, like a local or regional Chinese Crested club, or in a specific pursuit, such as obedience, tracking or hunting tests. There are all-breed clubs for all-dog enthusiasts; they sponsor special training days, seminars on topics like grooming or handling or lectures on breeding or canine genetics. There are also clubs that specialize in certain types of dogs, like herding dogs, hunting dogs, companion dogs, etc.

A parent club is the national organization, sanctioned by the AKC, which promotes and safeguards its breed in the country. The American Chinese Crested Club was formed in 1979 and can be contacted on the Internet at www.crestedclub.org. The parent club holds an annual national specialty show, usually in a different city each year, in which many of the country's top dogs, handlers and breeders gather to compete. At a specialty show, only members of a single breed are invited to participate. There are also Group specialties, in which all members of a Group are invited. For more information about dog clubs in your area, contact the AKC at www.akc.org on the Internet or write them at their Raleigh, NC address.

### How Shows Are Organized
Three kinds of conformation shows are offered by the AKC. There is the all-breed show, in which all AKC-recognized breeds can compete; the specialty show, which is for one breed only and usually sponsored by the breed's parent club and the group show, for all breeds in one of the AKC's seven groups. The Chinese Crested competes in the Toy Group.

For a dog to become an AKC champion of record, the dog must earn 15 points at shows. The points must be awarded by at least three different judges and must include two "majors" under different judges. A "major" is a three-, four- or five-point win, and the number of points per win is determined by the number of dogs competing in the show on that day. (Dogs that are absent or are excused are not counted.) The number of points that are awarded varies from breed to breed. More dogs are needed to attain a major in more popular breeds, and fewer dogs are needed in less popular breeds. Yearly, the AKC evaluates

A small breed like the Chinese Crested is examined on a table so that the judge can get a closer look.

the number of dogs in competition in each division (there are 14 divisions in all, based on geography) and may or may not change the numbers of dogs required for each number of points. For example, a major in Division 2 (Delaware, New Jersey and Pennsylvania) recently required 17 dogs or 16 bitches for a three-point major, 29 dogs or 27 bitches for a four-point major and 51 dogs or 46 bitches for a five-point major. The Chinese Crested attracts numerically proportionate representation at all-breed shows.

Only one dog and one bitch of each breed can win points at a given show. There are no "co-ed" classes except for champions of record. Dogs and bitches do not compete against each other until they are champions. Dogs that are

The multi-titled Int. and Am. Ch. Gingery's Krimson 'N' Clover is the only Chinese Crested to be awarded an AKC and International Best in Show award. A Sire of Distinction, he was #2 Crested in the US in 1998 and Top Crested in Europe.

> **READ ALL ABOUT IT**
> There are different ways to find out about dog shows in your area. The American Kennel Club's monthly magazine, the *American Kennel Gazette,* is accompanied by the *Events Calendar,* this magazine is available through subscription. You can also look on the AKC's and your parent club's websites for information and check the event listings in your local newspaper. Likewise, interested owners should subscribe to *Dog World* magazine as well as *Dogs in Review.*

not champions (referred to as "class dogs") compete in one of five classes. The class in which a dog is entered depends on age and previous show wins. First there is the Puppy Class (sometimes divided further into classes for 6- to 9-month-olds and 9- to 12-month-olds); next is the Novice Class (for dogs that have no points toward their championship and whose only first-place wins have come in the Puppy Class or the Novice Class, the latter class limited to three first places); then there is the American-bred Class (for dogs bred in the US); the Bred-by-Exhibitor Class (for dogs handled by their breeders or by immediate family members of their breeders) and the Open Class (for any non-champions). Any dog may enter the Open class, regardless of age or win history, but to be competitive the dog should be older and have ring experience.

The judge at the show begins judging the male dogs in the Puppy Class(es) and proceeds through the other classes. The judge awards first through fourth place in each class. The first-place winners of each class then compete with one another in the Winners Class to determine Winners Dog. The judge then starts over with the bitches, beginning with the Puppy Class(es) and proceeding up to the Winners Class to award Winners Bitch, just as he did with the dogs. A Reserve Winners Dog and Reserve Winners Bitch are also selected; they could be awarded the points in the case of a disqualification.

The Winners Dog and Winners Bitch are the two that are awarded the points for their breed. They then go on to compete with any champions of record (often called "specials") of their breed that are entered in the show. The champions may be dogs or bitches; in this class, all are shown together. The judge reviews the Winners Dog and Winners Bitch along with all of the champions to select the Best of Breed winner. The Best of Winners is selected between the Winners Dog and Winners Bitch; if one of these two is selected Best of Breed as well, he or she is automatically determined Best of Winners. Lastly, the judge selects Best of Opposite Sex to the Best of Breed winner. The Best of Breed winner then goes on to the Group competition.

At a Group or all-breed show, the Best of Breed winners from each breed are divided into their respective groups to compete against one another for Group One through Group Four. Group One (first place) is awarded to the dog that best lives up to the ideal for his breed as described in the standard. A Group judge, therefore, must have a thorough working knowledge of many breed standards. After placements have been made in each Group, the seven Group One winners (from the Sporting Group, Toy Group, Hound Group, etc.) compete against each other for the top honor, Best in Show.

Another top Powderpuff, this is Ch. Gingery's Eclair, a national specialty winner, handled by Victor Helu.

# My Chinese Crested

PUT YOUR PUPPY'S FIRST PICTURE HERE

Dog's Name _____

Date _____ Photographer _____